INSIDE THE MIND OF VLADIMIR PUTIN

MICHEL ELTCHANINOFF

Inside the Mind of Vladimir Putin

HURST & COMPANY, LONDON

First published in French by Actes Sud as *Dans la tête de Vladimir Poutine* in 2015.
This updated English edition published in the United Kingdom in 2018 by
C. Hurst & Co. (Publishers) Ltd.,
41 Great Russell Street, London, WC1B 3PL

Printed in the United Kingdom

Distributed in the United States, Canada and Latin America by
Oxford University Press, 198 Madison Avenue, New York, NY 10016,
United States of America.

A Cataloguing-in-Publication data record for this book
is available from the British Library.

ISBN: 9781849049337

This book is printed using paper from registered sustainable
and managed sources.

www.hurstpublishers.com

CONTENTS

CONTENTS

ACKNOWLEDGEMENTS

For their help and advice, many thanks to Galia Ackerman, Alexis Berelowitch, Wolfram Eilenberger, the whole team at *Philosophie Magazine*, Alexey Kozyrev, Sergei Khazov-Cassia, Bernard Marchadier, Ilya Platov, Constantin Sigov, Cyrille Sollogoub, and Matthieu Sollogoub—not forgetting my publisher, always attentive and warm, Michel Parfenov of Actes Sud. For their encouragement and their support, thanks to Élisabeth and to my children, André, Rébecca and Alexandre.

The origins of this book are to be found in an article published in no. 80 of *Philosophie Magazine (June 2014)*.

ACKNOWLEDGEMENTS

For much help [illegible]

INTRODUCTION

PUTIN AND PHILOSOPHY

Russia, early January 2014. The top officials, the regional governors and the senior functionaries of the United Russia party have just received an unusual New Year's gift from the president's office: works of philosophy. Ivan Ilyin's *Our Mission*, Nikolai Berdyaev's *The Philosophy of Inequality*, Vladimir Solovyov's *The Justification of the Good*—treatises by nineteenth- and twentieth-century Russian thinkers. If Gogol were to return from the dead, he would pen descriptions of these venerable party figures, accustomed to fashionable restaurants and expensive cars, toiling over the pages of sibylline speculation. They have no choice but to spend their evenings pulling their hair out like this; the president himself has recently quoted these authors in important speeches, and they now must try to understand what he meant. The most persistent among them will have found some strangely familiar ideas in these books, the past resonating with the present: the role of the nation's guide in an authentic democracy, the importance of being conservative, the need to anchor morality in religion, the historic mission of the Russian people against the age-old [timeless] hostility of the West, and so on.

In February 2014, some of these officials—those from the Ministry of Internal Affairs and the Kremlin's social affairs departments—attended compulsory conferences on the theme of conservatism. In March, it was the turn of United Russia's functionaries to be forced to attend classes at the State University.[1] This remedial Philosophy course was shaken by a historic event at the end of that month, the annexation of Crimea—but that was no reason to abandon it; quite the opposite. Proof of this came with the 2014 Tavrida International Youth Forum, held between 10 and 20 August in the newly conquered Crimea, where intellectuals gathered to explain to their young audience the intellectual origins and present-day reality of the 'conservative turn' inaugurated by Vladimir Putin. Among them was a professor at Moscow's prestigious State University, Boris Mezhuev, who outlined to a packed lecture theatre the country's great choice over its destiny: 'To build herself up as a separate civilization ... or to think of herself as the conservative saviour of Europe.'[2] Several historians of philosophy, specialists in Russian thought, were present alongside Mezhuev, while at the same moment, in a magnificent seaside palace (the former residence of Alexander III), other philosophers were discussing 'Conservative Thought in Russia' or 'The return of Crimea to Russia as a new stage in the construction of the Russian state: from the decline of the 1980s and '90s to a phase of consolidation'. Philosophy was to be found everywhere in Russia in 2014, and the president himself had left his mark on this movement by quoting thinkers.

Could it be that Putin is a philosophy fanatic? Hardly. The man prefers history, literature and, above all, sport. He is no scholar. He likes to recall his youth as a thug and spy rather than his law studies at St Petersburg State University. He demonstrates as often as possible that he prefers the great outdoors and physical exploits to libraries, and when he does mention philosophy, it is generally to mock those he sees as abstract hair splitters, or to admit his own ignorance. Otherwise, he may understand it, as do many Russians, in the sense of some great Eastern wisdom. He is happy to quote Lao Tzu, a 'great oriental philosopher',[3] and considers that the art of judo, which he practises, is the true philosophy. In short, nobody would dare make Putin out to be an intellectual.

Nor does he aspire, as a political leader, to impose a state ideology in the Soviet way. In 'Russia at the Turn of the Millennium', the programmatic document that he published on his accession to the interim presidency on New Year's Eve 1999, he distanced himself from the communist past: 'I am against the restoration in Russia of an official state ideology in any form. There should be no forced civil accord in a democratic Russia.'[4] He has since repeated himself with regularity on this point: 'I do not think that we need a dominant ideology and philosophy. But the state can, of course, be led by a philosopher—so long as he shares this vision of things.'[5] Putin has nothing against philosophers per se, but he rejects the figure of a Platonic philosopher king.

Finally, and above all, Vladimir Putin is a realist. He adapts his discourse according to circumstance and refuses to be bound by any ideological shackles. He wishes to retain the initiative and is surrounded by a horde of speechwriters who offer him multiple and shifting philosophical references to draw on. From former presidential advisers to commentators and intellectuals, everyone I've interviewed has challenged the idea of a 'Putin philosophy' as too simplistic. But one detail is significant. After denying that Putin possesses or applies a precise philosophical theory, they all began to enumerate the names of the great thinkers who, they believe, inform his actions and his vision of the world, explaining how Putin uses one or another aspect of their theories.

In reality, Putin is influenced by certain philosophical ideas, and this is apparent in his words and deeds. He's what might be termed a 'fundamental Soviet'. Like all citizens of the USSR, he was brought up on a quasi-religious respect for books and the great names of culture. In the Soviet Union, as in federal Russia today, nobody made fun of either culture or philosophy, which all students had to tackle at university, irrespective of their course. During his studies in the 1970s, Vladimir

Putin learned the names and doctrines of major thinkers, both Russian and foreign. Moreover, on the fall of the Berlin Wall, when he returned from the GDR after a five-year mission for the KGB (State Security Committee), the way that publishing had flourished during his absence certainly took him by surprise. A few years of perestroika had witnessed many authors being republished, or published for the first time—religious philosophers, émigré thinkers, eminent foreign authors, hitherto banned. Philosophy was very fashionable at that time, and in 1994 Solzhenitsyn returned to Russia, taking ideas thought to have disappeared and giving them new life. Putin's birthplace, St Petersburg, was an intellectual capital, with many more or less dissident philosophers living there, and it is possible that he may have encountered some of them. In any case, he must have been struck by the effervescent atmosphere of the period, especially as a specialized section of the KGB was following the intellectual debates shaping society. To watch a passionate argument over Soviet propaganda's distortion or denial of some part of Russian culture, he only had to switch on his television.

In a country divided into anti-communist democrats, more or less pro-Soviet nationalists and those nostalgic for the USSR, Putin needed ideological reference points once he had reached the presidency in 2000, to appear both pragmatic and flexible. He wanted to reassure his fellow citizens of the solidity of his thinking and programme, believing that the people needed to hear a discourse of structured narrative. The nation had to be galvanized in order to reconstruct the country and give clear direction to state officials. In a political system where the decision-making process is always very opaque, each of his words was bound to be closely scrutinized. When Putin quoted a particular philosopher in his speeches, notably in his major addresses to the nation or to parliament, it was no accident.

Putin has evolved since 2000. His convictions haven't changed, but he has increasingly dared to express them as they have crystallized and benefited from new meanings. His second presidential mandate, from 2004 to 2008, was characterized by a clear sense of tension, while the third, starting in 2012, began unambiguously on a note of revenge—against those protesting his return to power, and against the West. He turned towards conservatism in 2013 and became an imperialist the following year. In 2015, he took action beyond his own borders and confronted the United States by launching an ongoing intervention in Syria. In 2016, he tried by various means to influence the US presidential election, thus becoming a key actor in American domestic politics. More and more clearly, President Putin has come to embody the revenge of those for whom the collapse of the USSR and its metamorphosis into a democracy have been unbearable. He also wishes to leave his mark for posterity; to achieve this, ideas that are deeply rooted in the country's history are indispensable. Whether he believes in them is secondary. Perhaps Vladimir Putin, like Dostoevsky's hero Dmitri Karamazov, is 'of a broad nature'—both sincerely idealistic and sincerely cynical.

Before exploring the philosophical trajectory of 'Putinism', we should say a few words concerning the president's entourage. Who talks philosophy with him? Who likes to tell him what they've been reading? Who makes him read texts that were written a hundred years ago, but seem to apply to the present-day situation? We should first mention two of Putin's historic advisers. Vladislav Surkov, considered by the press as Putin's 'Rasputin', took a brief step back but has not lost his influence. This talented creator of the concept of 'sovereign democracy', an expert in 'political technologies' who created ad hoc political parties and youth movements, has become the president's adviser on Ukrainian affairs. Gleb Pavlovsky, on the other hand, who provided Putin with ideas in the 2000s during the period of 'managed democracy', is no longer part of the president's intellectual entourage. Putin, according to my interviewees, does not read newspapers and does not consult the Internet, which he distrusts. He is informed by memos sent to him, or the red files left on his desk by staff.

Who provides Putin with the information he needs? Firstly, friends and allies from the *siloviki* clan, mostly originating from the army, the police and the secret services, and often, like him, from St Petersburg. Comparing the sources and declarations of Russian interviewees, we can identify half a dozen individuals who are regularly close to the president in policy matters: Alexander Bortnikov, director of the FSB since 2008; Alexander Bastrykin, president of the Investigative Committee of Russia, a criminologist and a very old associate of Putin; Igor Sechin, another St Petersburger very close to Putin and head of the Rosneft oil company, suspected of being among those responsible for the detention of Mikhail Khordorkovsky and considered 'the third man in power' by the *Financial Times* in 2010 (after Putin and Medvedev); Yuri Kovalchuk, an oligarch heavily involved in banking and the media; Vladimir Yakunin, president of Russian Railways until August 2015; Minister of Defence Sergey Shoygu; and, to a lesser extent, Dmitry Rogozin, deputy prime minister in charge of the military-industrial sector, who was very active during the Ukrainian crisis. Since 2015–16, a reshuffle of top officials has taken place, and some among the faithful have been sidelined. Sergei Ivanov, head of the presidential administration from 2011, was replaced in the summer of 2016 by a discreet forty-year-old, Anton Vaino, a strange character who is a follower of the Russian mineralogist and chemist Vladimir Vernadsky (1863–1945), who invented the concept of the 'noosphere'—the sphere of human thought. Vaino is working on the development of a 'nooscope', 'the first device allowing the study of humanity's collective consciousness'.[6] On the other hand, Russians have also witnessed the return to the presidential fold of a former prime minister from the Yeltsin era, the 'liberal' Sergey Kirienko. This development has led certain political commentators to predict a softening of the regime's stance towards the West—was Kirienko not a friend of Boris Nemtsov, who was murdered near the Kremlin in February 2015? They have equally observed the promotion of Alexei Dyumin, whom Putin appointed governor of the Tula district in February 2016; he is sometimes depicted as the president's heir-in-waiting.

Among these former and current presidential intimates, the most involved in studying Russian thought and a conservative worldview is Vladimir Yakunin. Having obtained a doctorate in political science, he has organized intellectual gatherings—at great expense—around the theme of 'Dialogue of Civilizations', and holds violently anti-Western views. Highly religious, he visits Jerusalem each year at Easter so as to bring back a flame from the 'Holy Fire' said to appear miraculously. He thus aspires to be one spearhead of a religious and moral renaissance in Russia. Finally, although not political figures, two other men seem to exercise influence on the Russian president's thinking. Firstly, the well-known filmmaker Nikita Mikhalkov has for two decades sought to personify the rebirth of a 'White Russia' after the fall of communism, and he must surely discuss what he's been reading with the president, who sometimes appears with him in public. We will see that it was probably Mikhalkov who first introduced Putin to the philosopher Ivan Ilyin. Secondly, Putin is said to have a confessor, Father Tikhon Shevkunov, a former student of Moscow's film school and now superior at the Sretensky Monastery in the city's centre. Powerful and feared, he is said to have real influence over the president.[7]

What emerges from these meetings, from these discussions of books read, from this shared vision of the world? A doctrine that for some years could only be obscurely guessed at is now taking shape more and more clearly. Impenetrable and unpredictable, just like Putin himself, it is complex. Yet to me, having read and reread the classics of Russian thought (sometimes in the original), having interviewed informed commentators and actors within Russia's intellectual life and having dissected Putin's speeches as president, it seems that a clear picture is starting to form. This doctrine operates on various levels: starting from a claimed Soviet heritage and a feigned liberalism, the first of these levels revolves around a conservative mind-set. The second level involves a theory of the 'Russian Way', while the third consists of an imperial dream inspired by Eurasianist thinkers. Put together, the whole sits under the rubric of a philosophy with scientific pretensions.

This hybrid and unstable doctrine promises all of us an unsettled future. Let us examine it more closely.

1

SOVIETS FIRST AND FOREMOST

Is Putin seeking to rebuild the USSR? His Eurasian Union project and his 2014 offensive in Ukraine seem to suggest as much. And if this is the case, does that mean he longs for the days of the Soviet Union? Let's examine the facts. If he is a Sovietophile, it is primarily out of loyalty to his roots. Vladimir Putin was born in Leningrad, the cradle of the Russian Revolution, in 1952. This half-starved and rundown city still bore the scars of a deadly German blockade that had lasted almost two and a half years. Stalin was still alive. Putin's father had fought and been wounded during the Second World War as a member of the NKVD, the political police in charge of prisoners and responsible for the execution of the high command's orders. An atheist and a skilled worker in a factory producing railway carriages, he had joined the Communist Party, and for several years was a member of his factory's party section. Putin's mother—who was religious—lived on menial jobs.

Putin's grandfather, meanwhile, had lived a much less ordinary life, at the heart of the communist regime. Just after his accession to the Russian presidency, Putin had to explain himself on this matter. 'What would your grandfather think of his grandson, having become a democratically elected president?' asked an American journalist. Putin's response was slightly embarrassed: 'The fact that my grandfather worked as a cook for Stalin says absolutely nothing about his political opinions. It was another country then, another life.'[1] His grandfather had cooked for Lenin before Stalin, and ended his days in a Party nursing home.

Yet despite the family's loyalist credentials, the young Vladimir was far removed from any Leninist fervour. From what we know about him—we only know what he has been willing to tell, as he's kept his biography under lock and key since attaining power[2]—Putin has never really believed in communism. He very rarely quotes Marx in speeches or interviews, and even when he does it is only to criticize him. During a meeting with leading cultural figures in August 2014, for instance, when his interlocutor quoted Marx and Engels he joked: 'It's the Germans who are guilty, it was they who forced them on us, by exporting their Marxism here...'[3] Putin often confirms that he has never believed in the ideal of a classless society: 'I was convinced that the idea of communism was nothing more than a beautiful story, but ... a dangerous one ... leading to an impasse that was both ideological and economic.'[4] This is a crucial point: working within the KGB, and perfectly familiar with the USSR's arrested development in relation to developed countries, Putin knew from 'the middle or end of the 1980s'[5] that the statist economic model was steadily moving towards collapse. As a young man he therefore presented himself as rather more liberal on the economic front, and even if he was not anti-communist, he—like many of his compatriots—set no store by the propaganda or dream of a classless society. Always pragmatic, he has noted the failure of the planned economy.

Yet Vladimir Putin fully shares the cardinal values of Soviet society. He perhaps does not have the same political convictions as his father or grandfather, but he stresses that he shares with them what matters most: patriotism. In the same interview about his family, he insisted: 'All the members of my family loved—love—Russia, showed themselves to be patriots towards my Fatherland and raised me precisely in that spirit.'[6] Indeed, he believes that what was taught in the Soviet Union, ahead of any communist ideology, was 'love of one's country'.[7]

Another fundamental value of Soviet society in which the young Putin immersed himself was military culture. In her chronicles of life in the USSR, the Belarusian writer Svetlana Alexievich emphasizes this trait, essential for understanding contemporary events: 'Our country was a military country, 70% of our economy was in the service of the army. And also our best minds. Physicians, mathematicians...' Everybody—men, women and children—were subject to 'military ideology'.[8] Education was militarist, and children were obliged to read war literature as preparation for self-sacrifice. Military service, with its atrocious humiliations and virile initiation ceremonies, constituted one of the most important moments in Soviet life. In general, the mood of all aspects of existence was martial, featuring parades, hero and martyr cults, and collective discipline. 'We thought that one day we would live well. Wait, put up with it ... Wait, be patient ... We spent our entire lives in barracks, in dormitories, in bunkhouses,' recalls Svetlana Alexievich.[9] Even today, across the entire ex-Soviet region a dry military efficiency marks the way civilians are talked about, the way that people address others. Moreover, observed one of the ordinary Soviets interviewed by Alexievich, in the grandiose struggle between the capitalist and communist worlds, 'there is no line between a state of peace and a state of war. We are always at war.'[10] Having grown up, several years after the end of the Second World War, in the 'Hero City' whose wartime legacy remains sacred, Vladimir Putin was a child of this everyday militarism. But he himself did not fight. He was born after the war, did not take part in the Soviet–Afghan War (1979–89), and by the time of the first Chechen conflict (1994–6) was already a highly placed functionary. As for the Second Chechen War, which began with an invasion in 1999, it was he who unleashed it. Putin seems to be all the more militaristic for never personally having known war. If he likes to project the image of a manly hero, it is because that image haunts him.

One important characteristic of this militarist culture has informed the philosophy of 'spontaneous history' common to many Soviets: it was the USSR that was first to halt the German advance, overcoming the enemy forces at Stalingrad and then forced their retreat to Berlin. Stalin, who had previously signed a pact with Hitler, then became the conflict's great victor in the eyes of the world. The culture of permanent war is also one of victory, and that, in the eyes of Soviet and Russian leaders, confers certain rights. At the beginning of his third mandate in 2012, in his intensifying glorification of the army (accompanied by a budget increase) Putin drew on the victory against Nazism to give Russia a sort of moral superiority in international relations. In his 2012 Victory Day speech, he proclaimed, 'We have an immense moral right: to defend our positions in a fundamental and lasting way. Because our country was the one subjected to the bulk of the Nazi offensive ... and it was our country that offered freedom to the peoples of the whole world.'[11] Nobody yet suspected that the traditional USSR rhetoric, contrasting the 'fascist' with the soldier as liberator of peoples, would reappear two years later in order to justify the 2014 intervention in Ukraine. But the argument itself was already in place.

* * *

Another Soviet institution has occupied a central place in Vladimir Putin's life: the KGB, renamed the FSB (Federal Security Service) after the collapse of the USSR. According to the legend that he himself first constructed and has carefully managed since, the sixteen-year-old apparently presented himself at the KGB's Leningrad headquarters in the late '60s, in order to defend his fatherland. He was advised first to undertake his studies, before being recruited several years later. In his authorized biographies and interviews, Putin has glamorized the romantic image of the spy, bold and incorruptible, and has sought to play down both the hundreds of thousands of victims of Stalin's secret police and the pitiless pursuit of dissidents and other 'deviants' in which he himself certainly took part. For Putin, the KGB-FSB was the elite corps of the Soviet fatherland. Where the communist leaders were corrupt, and their actions shackled by ideology, the secret police understood the backwardness of the Communist Bloc and acted as the spearhead of a national renaissance.

Simply put, the ideal is a political police in power, liberated from the tutelage of the Party; on becoming president, Putin stated very clearly that: 'The KGB was an ideological organization, serving the interests of a party in power—the Communist Party of the Soviet Union. Now, thank God, we no longer have a party in power and or a statist communist ideology.'[12] Henceforth, then, the FSB can accomplish its mission with a free hand: 'To defend the interests of the state.'[13] Putin moreover extols the professional qualities developed by spies: 'The skills of working with people: knowing how to listen, knowing how to understand.'[14] This ability to win his interlocutor's trust, and adapt in response to him, has often been singled out by those who have met Putin. Did he not, in his youth, define himself as a 'specialist in human relations'?[15]

* * *

Such opposition to Marxist-Leninist ideology, combined with unstinting loyalty to the Soviet Union and one of its principal institutions, the secret police, makes Putin's position on the Soviet century accommodating to say the least. We can say with certainty that he's never wanted to facilitate the Soviet past being called into question. Boris Yeltsin, who became the first democratically elected Russian president in 1991, had already rejected the former dissident Vladimir Bukovsky's proposal to organize a 'Nuremberg trial' of the Soviet leadership. At the start of his own presidency nine years later, Putin did not seem for a second to envisage any such possibility. Nor was there any question for him of initiating a memory project to examine the communist century and its repression, which would have prevented the surreptitious rebirth of its values and discourse. He considered that the Russian people suffered enough in the free but unstable decade that followed the demise of the USSR. His prioritisation of social stability has allowed him to avoid any examination of the collective conscience, and he argued cleverly that

> seeking clarity about communism does not mean organizing purges and pursuing people on the sole grounds that they may have been members of the Communist Party or might have worked in certain militarized organizations linked to the party. That would be the biggest of mistakes. That would sow discord throughout society.[16]

It is enough, he continued, simply to get rid of communist ideology and the one-party state.

At the same time as professing this balanced position, Putin also rehabilitated certain aspects of Soviet culture early in his presidency. His solution to the extremely sensitive question of national symbols was to offer something for everyone. The Russian flag would be neither the tsarist nor the Soviet version, but the white, blue and red flag of the Russia liberated from imperial rule, the banner of the February 1917 revolution. The words of the national anthem were to be rewritten, but by the man who had composed the Soviet anthem: Sergey Mikhalkov, a well-known writer in favour during the communist period, and father of the filmmaker Nikita

Mikhalkov. The tune would remain the same as in the Soviet period. The coat of arms, the double-headed eagle, would allude to imperial Russia, while the military flag would remain that of the Red Army. 'Do we have nothing other than Stalinist camps and repression to remind us of the Soviet epoch?' he asked, before listing the great names of space exploration to justify the return of Soviet symbols.[17] Claiming that a majority of citizens favoured retaining the music of the Soviet anthem, Putin concluded with an emotional argument:

> If we agree with the idea that symbols from past ages, including the Soviet era, should not be used, then we must concede that whole generations of our fellow citizens, our mothers and fathers, led useless and absurd lives, that they lived those lives for nothing. I cannot accept this with either my head or my heart.'[18]

In the name of national reconciliation, historical continuity and filial piety, Vladimir Putin has definitively forbidden any critical reassessment of a past that is both recent and tragic. The most recent illustration of this position was the discomfort that seemed to grip the authorities as the centenary of the 1917 revolution approached. The Kremlin, not wanting to face the enduring divisions on the subject within Russian society, left organization of the commemorations to the Russian Historical Society. According to a VTsIOM opinion poll of 20 April 2016, 31 per cent of Russians considered that Lenin did more good than harm, while

23 per cent thought the opposite.[19] A Levada poll on 14 February 2017 found that 32 per cent of interviewees thought that 'the February revolution was a step on the path to the glorious socialist revolution of October,' embracing the Soviet interpretation of the event, whereas 19 per cent adopted the monarchist view that 'the February revolution weakened the country.' Only 11 per cent agreed with the proposition that 'if not for the October coup, the February revolution would have allowed Russia to move towards progress and democracy'[20]—the so-called liberal version of this history.

Since the collapse of the USSR in 1991, controversy has also surrounded Lenin's mausoleum, which has pride of place in Moscow's Red Square. Neither Yeltsin nor, so far, Putin has dared to move the remains of the father of the revolution, for fear of unleashing the fury of those nostalgic for the Soviet system. According to an opinion poll of April 2016, 36 per cent of Russians favour the idea that Lenin should be buried as soon as possible in his family's cemetery plot, but 32 per cent would rather he was left in his mausoleum. On this question, too, the powers that be are walking on eggshells.

The theme of the revolution is also an irritant to Putin, who believes he stabilized Russia after the turbulent 1990s and hopes to avoid a 'colour revolution' of political protest (in the style of Georgia's 2003 Rose Revolution and Ukraine's Orange Revolution in 2004–5). As such, he is caught in a paradox: though anti-revolutionary himself, he has no objection to serving as the president of those who long for the USSR. He prefers, then, not to dig too deeply into the founding moment of 1917. In his address to the Federal Assembly on 1 December 2016, he declared:

> The centenary is an opportunity to focus once more on the causes and the nature of the Russian Revolution. ... Russian society needs objective, honest and deep analyses of these events. On the other hand, it is absolutely intolerable to want to provoke divisions, hatred and vilifications and to make our relationship with the past more difficult. We cannot speculate on tragedies.

This last remark was aimed at certain historians and NGOs wishing to carry out real research into the Soviet period, such as Memorial, whose objective is to remember the victims of Stalinism and which is accordingly a target for relentless legal harassment. Putin fears that two pillars of his support may yet tear each other apart, since he is propped up both by 'reds' who yearn for the USSR and conservative and Orthodox 'whites' united around the idea of empire and national greatness.

This posture of reconciliation has guided the president's policy since he took power, but it has also sometimes forced him into awkward contortions. In the same speech, for instance, he quoted a sentence by the philosopher and religious thinker Aleksei Losev (1893–1988): 'We know the thorny road our country has travelled. We know the long and tiring years of struggle, want and suffering, but for our homeland's sons, this is all their native, inalienable heritage.' These words might lead one to believe that Losev, who was hostile to the Russian Revolution, embraced reconciliation by placing love of country above the inherited divisions of history. Yet what Putin failed to mention was that Losev served several years in prison camps in the 1930s and was only published after Stalin's death. Through this omission, he transformed a victim of repression into a propagandist for Soviet patriotism.

This mixture of sentimentalism, desire for political reconciliation, and a skewed view of history has gradually enabled Putin to crystallize his vision of the USSR. He began modestly, considering the effects of its collapse in the first of his 'Direct Line' appearances (a major Q&A television broadcast): 'Anyone who doesn't miss the Soviet Union has no heart. And anyone who wants it back has no brain.'[21] Several years later, during his highly formal official speech to the two chambers of the Federal Assembly, Putin produced an even more emphatic phrase, one that would become famous: 'First and foremost, it is worth acknowledging that the demise of the Soviet Union was the greatest geopolitical catastrophe of the century.'[22] Not the Second World War, then, nor the Russian Revolution, nor Stalin's seizure of Central and Eastern Europe. But again, the president took pleasure in refuting accusations that he lamented the loss of one of the twentieth century's bloodiest dictatorships. Two years later, in 2007, he explained to *TIME* magazine that he had spoken those words in a humanitarian spirit:

> What did the collapse of the Soviet Union mean? 25 million Soviet citizens who were ethnic Russians found themselves outside Russia's borders and no one gave them any thought. This is equivalent to the population of a large European country. They suddenly found themselves foreigners, without ever having been asked about what they themselves wanted. ... So, 25 million people found themselves abroad without any means, in a climate of rising nationalism and in a situation where they couldn't return to Russia, their historic homeland, and couldn't even see their relatives, because they did not have the money to buy a plane or train ticket. They don't have apartments in Russia. They have nowhere to live and no jobs. Is this not a tragedy? This is what I meant [when I said those words]. I had in mind not the political aspect of the Soviet Union's collapse but the humanitarian aspect. And was that not a tragedy? Of course it was, and a great tragedy too.[23]

Even with these words, those who read the interview likely would not have expected Putin to come to the military aid of some such 'stranded' citizens seven years later. It was not until then that the crux of Putin's thoughts on the USSR's disintegration became clear. His declaration to the Assembly in 2005 had been intended as objective and humanitarian, but in his major speech on 18 March 2014, celebrating the recent annexation of

Crimea, the president added an adverb full of meaning to his usual formula: '*Unfortunately*, what seemed impossible became a reality. The USSR fell apart.'[24] There was a simple reason for Putin allowing himself this value judgement after fifteen years in power: with the military operation in Ukraine, he had now begun to right the wrong.

* * *

The idea that the downfall of the USSR was not only a human catastrophe but also a historical error to be corrected was not, it must be said, new, and in the case of Putin, consistent and highly suggestive hints of this argument could already be detected before the intervention in Ukraine. Firstly, Putin has always stated that the end of communism created a serious problem, that of the 'ideological void'.[25] Of course, as we have seen, he has insisted that he is 'opposed to the restoration of an official ideology of the Russian state', emphasizing that such a restoration can only be 'voluntary'.[26] Yet he has done everything possible to encourage the emergence of a replacement ideology containing all the aspects that he judges to have been positive in the Soviet system—everything apart from the idea of communism itself.

Secondly, at the same time as he first pronounced this view, just before his appointment as Boris Yeltsin's prime minister in 1999, Russia was feeling humiliated by NATO's military interventions in Serbia and Kosovo.

This attack on one of Russia's historic allies, with no mandate from the UN Security Council and carried out on moral grounds, provoked outrage among the Russian people and their leaders. My conviction is that Putin's political career was shaped from that moment on by a plan to take revenge for this episode.[27] In any case, when Russia invaded Georgia in 2008 or intervened in Ukraine in 2014, the Russian authorities deployed humanitarian rhetoric in an ostentatious, almost parodic manner, like a bitterly ironic 'return to sender'. A section of the ex-Soviet elite experienced the 1990s as a series of affronts inflicted by Western democracies they viewed as brutal and hypocritical.

Thirdly, the 2000s and 2010s saw the steady rehabilitation of the most criminal figures of Soviet history, with Stalin at the head of the pack. Since 2002, in keeping with the logic of the age, Putin has offered a balanced judgement: 'Stalin, of course, was a dictator. There is no doubt about it. ... The problem is that it was under his specific leadership that the country won the Second World War. That victory is broadly connected to his name. And to ignore this state of affairs would be stupid.'[28] Through history manuals, posters, commemorations and plans to rename Volgograd as Stalingrad, today's Russia is rehabilitating the dictator. In other words, Putin has moved on from sentimental nostalgia and humanitarian concerns to a pro-Soviet and pro-Stalinist rereading of the Soviet century. One final example of this is the comeback of another symbol of Soviet terror: the sinister Felix Dzerzhinsky, founder of the Cheka (secret police), whose statue used to stand in Lubyanka Square. On 22 September 2014, the Ministry of the Interior's website announced that an internal operational security division within the Ministry was to 're-adopt the name of the Dzerzhinsky Division'. The decree had been signed by the president himself. In 1991, the first symbolic act of the democratic revolution that overthrew the communist regime had been to topple Dzerzhinsky's statue from its plinth. The time is now ripe, it seems, for his comeback. In September 2017, to mark 140 years since his birth, a statue of Dzerzhinsky was unveiled in the town of Kirov, 800 kilometres from Moscow. A few days later, a Dzerzhinsky museum was opened in the same region in the village of Kai, where he was once exiled.[29]

Beyond this return to the past, Putin's way of thinking remains very Soviet. On this point, I interviewed the political commentator and journalist Alexander Morozov, one of the best observers of Russian political life. Editor-in-chief of the website *Russky Zhurnal* (Russian Journal), he recognizes in Putin specific thought structures:

> One sees in his vocabulary that he relies on the terminology of late Soviet ideology, no longer really Marxist, which was that of his youth. It can be seen in his way of describing the West, which he equates to anything west

> of the Russian Federation, without understanding that the notion of the West today is global and refers equally to South Asia. He has also retained, in his public discourse, a totally Soviet stance as regards international organizations. He is convinced that world centres do exist—the nuclear powers—and that beside them, international organizations are only of very secondary importance. Finally, one can see that he has retained a Soviet characterization of Russia's power, in a military and political sense. There's a sort of contempt for small nations that he doesn't attempt to conceal, especially toward those bordering Russia.[29]

This way of thinking now forms the basis for both his conception of history, and his approach to policy.

2

KANT, PETER THE GREAT AND THE PHILOSOPHY OF JUDO

Though Putin has never been able to rid himself of his Soviet background, or indeed wanted to do so, in the 1990s and early 2000s he nonetheless dressed himself up as a liberal, presenting himself as both a democrat keen to help his country re-embrace Western norms and an advocate of the free market. Was this posture sincere? And, if so, why did Putin's portrait of the pro-European Peter the Great, hung in his St Petersburg mayoral office in the early 1990s, come off his office walls in the Kremlin ten years later?

The concept of Putin as a liberal is based on various hypotheses. He was born in Leningrad, the former St Petersburg, constructed at the beginning of the eighteenth century at the behest of Peter I, who wanted to make it 'a window on Europe'. Indeed, this city that became Russia's capital, 'the most abstract and intentional city in the world' according to Dostoyevsky,[1] played a major role in the Enlightenment movement. Diderot spent time there as a counsellor to the Empress Catherine the Great. In contrast with Moscow, a religious and patriarchal city closed to Europe and symbolizing links with the country's deepest traditions, St Petersburg represented administrative, political and ideological rationality. And when the Bolsheviks chose to make Moscow capital once again, St Petersburg, which became Petrograd and then Leningrad, was far from the Kremlin, embodying a pro-European counterculture. It is well known that Putin is very attached to the city of his birth, which he had widely renovated to celebrate its tercentenary in 2003. It is also common knowledge that he took with him to the Kremlin a large number of his former St Petersburger comrades, not least Dmitry Medvedev. When asked in 2001 to name his favourite historical figures, Putin listed Stolypin, Nicholas II's iron-fisted prime minister, but also the two great emperors and builders of St Petersburg, 'Peter the Great and Catherine II'.[2]

A second possible source of Putin's supposed liberalism could be his law studies, carried out in the city's magnificent university across the River Neva from St Isaac's Cathedral and the 'Bronze Horseman', the statue of Peter the Great by Étienne-Maurice Falconet. A lawyer's accession to the presidency in 2000 encouraged the image of a leader concerned with installing the rule of law and strengthening the country's democratic institutions. At the law faculty, the young Putin had been receptive to Western republican thought. The political analyst Alexander Morozov supports this view: 'I've been told that Putin was a serious student and that at St Petersburg University's law faculty he studied Kant, Hobbes and Locke. He even quoted Kant, author of the *Critique of Pure Reason*, in a speech written for the city's mayor, Anatoly Sobchak.'[3] Indeed, the president has mentioned Immanuel Kant's name several times in official speeches—whereas Plato, Descartes, Leibnitz, Rousseau and Hegel have been absent. Kant's *What is Enlightenment?*, with its celebrated 'Dare to know!' call to human emancipation through understanding, marked the apogee of eighteenth-century thought.

Yet the use that Putin makes of Kant has more to do with a political challenge. The philosopher was born and lived his whole life in the capital of western Prussia, Königsberg. This city, absorbed by the USSR in 1945, became Kaliningrad and has since been a Russian exclave situated between Lithuania and Poland. After the fall of the USSR, it became a centre for smuggling of all sorts, before developing as an outpost of new Russian power. On a 2005 visit to this anomalous territory, in a bid to 'degermanify' the philosopher a little, Putin asserted: 'Of course, Kant is first and foremost a great figure of the German Enlightenment, but he is more than that. Thanks to his considerable contribution to global culture, he is among that category of people we can call citizens of the world.'[4] He even called him 'a shared compatriot' of Germans and Russians.[5] Putin has also celebrated Kant as a theoretician of the principles of modern democracy and peace between nations. He has emphasized on several occasions that Kant was the author of *Perpetual Peace*, a work where he laid out the conditions that would allow us to look forward to the progressive extinction of wars. Among these is the presence of a republican constitution through which peoples could check and, most of the time, prevent aggressive adventures on the part of their leaders. In the company of his friend German Chancellor Gerhard Schröder, the Russian president waxed eloquent:

> I remind you that Kant protected such basic concepts of the modern world as freedom, and equality for everyone before the law. He stood against any segregation on the basis of religion and ethnicity.
>
> I remind you also that Kant was a categorical opponent to resolving international arguments through war. And we are trying to adhere to his doctrine in this regard. I believe that the vision Kant has outlined must be enacted by our generation. Just like his doctrine concerning the division of authority, which has already been realized, his doctrine on the peaceful solution of international disputes can and must be implemented. It's on these basic principles that we will build our relationships with the Europeans and with other foreign countries.[6]

Today, Putin seems altogether less Kantian.

References to Kant were very common at the time of communism's demise, and the vision of a world rid of dictatorships and living under the rule of law, democracy and the free market was often evoked at international summits. In the same period, Putin was cutting his teeth in politics with one of the main leaders of post-Soviet Russia, the mayor of St Petersburg Anatoly Sobchak (1937–2000), who was thought to be the most fervent of liberals. Putin always depicted himself as ready to come to the aid of his former mentor, and he appeared particularly affected by the latter's suspicious death in February 2000. Yet Sobchak's liberalism is a matter of debate. Was he not rather, as Masha Gessen suggests in her biography of Putin,[7] a communist apparatchik masquerading as a liberal? She also claims that the proclaimed liberalism of Putin, who at the time was a KGB reserve officer charged with both supporting and monitoring Sobchak, concealed a hatred of 'democrats'.[8] Whatever the case, in the years after Sobchak's sudden and mysterious death, Putin has not portrayed his mentor as an apostle of absolute political liberty, but as a supporter of order. To the former Polish dissident Adam Michnik, Putin summed up Sobchak's main political tenets as follows: 'There is much freedom, but there are few democratic institutions. But now, freedom of expression, political parties working freely, are referring to those institutions. ... Democracy is not anarchy, it's not "anything goes".'[9] The world has seen more liberal political theories than this.

Even if Putin's liberalism is limited by his desire for order, it cannot be denied that during the early years of his presidency he demonstrated an exemplary form of Occidentalism, at least on the surface. As Alexander Morozov explains, 'in the first half of his reign, his political philosophy was in line with Western standards. Political projects concerning "the specific Russian way" didn't interest him. He wanted to align his country with worldwide norms in the domains of education, the economy, legislation and property rights.'[10] At the time, Putin certainly rejected any discourse of a 'Russian idea', of a civilizing project separate from the Western model. In 2002, again in response to a question from dissident Adam Michnik about Putin's vision of Russia's historic role and eventual expansionist designs, the president made himself very clear: 'The economic development of the enormous territories that find themselves under the control of the Russian Federation is a joint task with Europe and other civilizations', within the perspective of a 'natural integration into political, economic and defensive structures among civilized countries'.[11] When asked whether Russia looks more towards Europe or Asia, his answer was unequivocal: 'From a geographical point of view, Russia is, of course, a Eurasian country. But … Russia is without any doubt a European country, because it is a country of European culture.'[12] There was no question of confrontation with the rest of the world: 'Who here could be interested in a confrontation between Russia and the rest of the world and with one of the most powerful states in the world—the United States? Whom could that interest? People like that don't exist!'[13]

At this point, then, Putin did not consider NATO as an enemy,[14] and he also assured his audience that Russia claimed no prerogative nor had imperialist ambitions concerning any particular geographical area: 'We have never proclaimed any region of the world as a zone of national interest.'[15] In other words, Russia had no mission to isolate itself from the rest of what Putin liked to call the 'civilized world'. During this first presidential term (2000–4), he repeatedly told anyone who would listen that Russia was fully European. '[We live in a country] that is an integral part of Europe and aspires to the status of European power.'[16] This was a civilizational union: 'Russia is a European country, above all in its way of thinking, its mentality, its culture.'[17] Its consequence was a Russian desire 'to act in the direction of judicial unification with Europe ... and to enlarge our cooperation in all fields'.[18] But what culture did Putin have in mind?

If he was remaining faithful to the Kantian spirit, he must have been thinking of the emergence of law, of critical thought, of the political, social and judicial structures facilitating human emancipation. In reality, though, his thought process was not at all clear. We have seen that Putin has often alluded to Kant, but normally in extremely specific contexts: defending Kaliningrad's annexation by the USSR or in meetings with German officials. In 2003, when asked the ritual question about Russia belonging to Europe, he replied, 'Russia is, of course, a European state, by both geography and mentality. What is Europe? It is the culture of Ancient Rome, of Ancient Greece, the culture of Byzantium, in other words of eastern Christianity.'[19] Europe, then, was primarily defined in terms of its historical, notably Christian, origins, and not by the philosophical-legal endeavours of more recent centuries. Here, Putin was no longer thinking in terms of progress, but of identity, which was to be protected. Moreover, he ruled out the possibility of Russia entering a European political entity, and in the same interview revealed a certain bitterness over Europe's advance towards the East—notably, the Baltic states, three former Soviet republics, would be joining the European Union in 2004. Putin then complained that 'sometimes the impression is created that Russia is being pushed onto the outer edge of European politics.'[20]

* * *

As early as 2003, then, a sense of resentment towards and an identitarian definition of Europe were already discernible, but their effects would not be felt until a decade later. By the end of 2012, Putin's way of talking about Europe had radically changed, the question of union replaced by the notion of possible *rapprochements*:

'As regards the possibility of Russia joining the EU, this is not realistic, as we well understand, neither from the territorial nor economic point of view. But what we ought to be able to do, in my view, is to look for paths of *rapprochement* and to develop synergies.'[21] From pro-Western liberalism early in the new millennium evolved the 'conservative turn', and a denial of Russia's intrinsic European destiny.

But perhaps there was something more than resentment behind this, something other than a gradual change of opinion on Europe. Putin's liberal and pro-European, even pro-Western, discourse has been counterbalanced by other forms of belief and action, according to somebody formerly close to the Russian president. The liberal economist Andrei Illarionov was Putin's chief economic adviser from 2000 until he resigned in 2005; he has since been a senior fellow at libertarian think-tank the Cato Institute, in Washington DC. He believes that the perception of Putin as a liberal, 'was widespread ... around the world and in Russia. But it was inaccurate', even though Putin surrounded himself with supporters of deregulation during his first term of office. 'To claim that he was liberal at the beginning and conservative later on doesn't really reflect his vision of things or his actions in that period.'[22] Firstly, in terms of the economy,

> he adopted a neutral economic model, prevalent in the West, neither to the left nor liberal in the classic sense

> and also not in the tradition of libertarian philosophy, which would have implied a minimization of the size and role of the state and of regulation as well as a lowering of taxation. He had an approach, let's say, that was just a little more liberal than the dominant global trend at the time.[23]

He was even less liberal from a political perspective, insists Illarionov. Looking back at the start of Putin's career in the democratic camp, he points out: 'Anatoly Sobchak was neither a liberal nor a democrat. He was a KGB collaborator. But Putin needed, at a particular point, to use Sobchak's liberal and democratic image'[24] in order to rise up the ranks. The aim of Putin and of the FSB, which had propelled him into power, was purely to 'infiltrate "democratic Russia". Putin passed himself off as a liberal but concealed his real views and pursued a different sort of politics.'[25] To prove his point, Illarionov lists the remarkable feats carried out in Putin's first weeks in power:

> As soon as he was nominated Yeltsin's prime minister, in August 1999, he initiated a military operation in Chechnya—an operation planned several months earlier. In September 1999 he gave the order to instigate explosions in Dagestan, which were, like those that followed, blamed on the Chechens in order to be able to attack them. In reality these explosions had been organized by the secret services in order to justify an intervention. Then came the deadly bombing of the

> Chechen republic, of the capital Grozny, which killed between 100,000 and 200,000 people, military and civilian. This was followed by the kidnapping and detention in solitary confinement of Andrei Babitsky, an independent journalist working at Radio Liberty. He would have been killed if a protest campaign hadn't succeeded in freeing him. Once Putin had taken over the presidency in 2000, he immediately removed the oligarch Vladimir Gusinsky in order to take over his NTV television group. He organized a campaign to force another oligarch, Boris Berezovsky, to flee and abandon his ORT TV channel. He thus took immediate control of the country's main media outlets. He was behind a campaign against businessmen who owned part of the Gazprom company and who were thrown in jail...[26]

As for the issue of national symbols, Illarionov is categorical: 'In the first year there was a terrible fight to have the Soviet anthem restored. Putin was the only one to support the idea. A good part of the presidential administration, me included, was fiercely against. He ended up imposing his views. The Soviet anthem returned.'[27]

On careful examination of Putin's words at the start of the 2000s, it becomes apparent that he wasn't saying the same thing to everyone. To his European friends he quoted Kant and professed Russia's profound Europeanness. Yet when he went to Asia—and during this period he developed a very active diplomatic relationship with the East—it was a different story. In China, for example, in Putin's first weeks as elected president, he condemned the West and its humanitarian policy—the humiliating memory of NATO's 1999 intervention in Kosovo was all too recent. He knew that by emphasizing this point he would win approval from the Chinese leadership, which does not tolerate others taking an interest in its 'internal affairs'. Putin considered that 'from time to time we encounter new threats, very dangerous concepts, like for example interference in another state's internal affairs on so-called humanitarian grounds.'[28] When asked whether he still kept a portrait of the Westernizing emperor Peter the Great in his office, he was almost apologetic: 'I have no portrait hanging in my office today, even if I did have a portrait of Peter I in my workplace in St Petersburg. ... I have great respect for Peter I as a reformer',[29] he added—in other words, not as a pro-Western leader. Putin's liberalism, it seems, varies according to longitude, and in the Far East dies out altogether.

* * *

Putin is not, in essence, a liberal. St Petersburg was not only Russia's European capital, but was also the city of imperial power and hierarchical authority. Kant, for Putin, is in reality nothing more than a name with which to win over European politicians. The personal philosophy of Putin the man, beyond his attachment to

Soviet greatness, originates neither in Paris nor Berlin—but in Japan. One of the means by which Putin achieves popularity, not only in Russia but also abroad, is his participation in judo. A former St Petersburg champion, he has widely distributed images of himself dressed in white judo uniform, looking powerful, focused, agile. In 2000, he declared that 'judo is not only a sport, but also ... a philosophy.'[30] He repeated his view in 2013: 'Judo brings together unique combat techniques and an original and profound philosophy', which 'cultivates the best human qualities'.[31]

In an interview with Japanese journalists, Putin remarked that the word judo means 'way of gentleness. ... It is a philosophy that prefers evolution to revolution. This philosophy', he believes, 'teaches us to make use of what we have and to value what we have',[32] strengths sufficient to overthrow one's adversary. He emphasized that the fundamentals of judo are 'respect for the opponent, whoever he may be. Respect for the elder, for one's master, a way of approaching problems that is not based on brute force, but on mastery, tactics and, of course, qualities of will.'[33]

This is the way Putin acted in the early years of his presidency. He made approaches to all possible partners, in the East and the West, showing respect and awaiting a reaction. The way of gentleness consists of winning the other person's trust, then observing him and working out what strength can be used to unbalance him. That is why Putin's liberalism is just one facet of his approach to problem solving; a way of reassuring those in the West while waiting for them to make a mistake.

3

THE PRESIDENT'S FIRST PHILOSOPHICAL LOVE

One Friday in September 2005, those revering the memory of White Russia[1] were in seventh heaven. On Paris's rue Daru, the moving prayer for the dead, *Memory Eternal*, was rising up to the vaulted ceiling of the Orthodox Alexander Nevsky Cathedral, sung by a choir that had come specially from Russia. The priests, from the Archdiocese of Russian Orthodox Churches in Western Europe, the Moscow Patriarchate and the Russian Orthodox Church Abroad—which still yearns for pre-revolutionary Russia—swung their incense burners. Noticeable among the 'Muscovites' was a young priest, Archimandrite Tikhon Shevkunov, head of a sumptuous monastery in the very centre of Moscow close to the FSB's headquarters, and said to be Putin's confessor. He is predicted a great future. In the front row were important individuals such as the Russian minister of culture or the Russian ambassador to France. But the star of the show was the filmmaker Nikita Mikhalkov, project manager of the event.

Those present were attending a service in honour of some recently exhumed human remains. The first belonged to Anton Denikin (1872–1947), a White Army general disinterred in New York, and his wife, taken from the Russian Cemetery at Sainte-Geneviève-des-Bois in the Parisian suburbs, where the writer Ivan Bunin, the dancer Rudolf Nureyev and the filmmaker Andrei Tarkovsky are among the notable buried. The other remains, arriving from Switzerland, belonged to a less well-known man: the Russian philosopher Ivan Ilyin (1883–1954).

Several days later, another ceremony took place in the cemetery of Moscow's Donskoy Monastery to rebury these three luminaries, with great pomp, close to Ivan Shmelyov (1873–1950), a Russian writer who migrated to France, and whose own mortal remains had been repatriated five years earlier. Nikita Mikhalkov delivered a fervent tribute to this symbol of national reconciliation between White and Red Russia. Then, several months later, the archives of Ivan Ilyin were returned from the United States to Russia. Businessmen close to the Kremlin—notably Victor Vekselberg—financed the operation, certainly at the president's express request, as part of a programme entitled 'For Reconciliation and Union', whose goal was to erase the social and cultural divisions born with the 1917 revolution. It was under the aegis of this programme that the remains of Denikin, Shmelyov and Ilyin were transferred to Moscow. According to Sergey Markov, a member of the Public Chamber charged with representing civil society from 2005, 'Vladimir Putin is apparently not indifferent to Ivan Ilyin.'[2] Archimandrite Shevkunov has gone one better, recounting how the president saw the miserable state of these White Russian figures' tombs, became indignant and resolved to do something about it.[3] It seems that Putin himself approved sketches of the planned new sepulchres, and, on 24 May 2009, when he had temporarily handed over the presidency to Dmitry Medvedev (2008–12), he personally laid flowers on the tombs. This was no chance event; Ivan Ilyin had become Putin's philosopher of choice, quoted in the most important of his speeches. More or less unknown in Russia during the Soviet period, and marginal even within the very rich Russian philosophy of inter-war emigration, it was Putin who established Ilyin's present-day popularity.

Yet it was indubitably Nikita Mikhalkov who first introduced him to Putin. We should recall that the actor and filmmaker, renowned in Russia and well-known around the world for films such as *Dark Eyes* and *Burnt by the Sun*, has played an increasingly prominent role in the media and politics since the fall of the USSR. He has also fallen in love with tsarist Russia. At the end of the Yeltsin era, when he seemed to be nursing presidential ambitions, Mikhalkov appeared in *The Barber of Siberia* as Alexander III, the conservative emperor of the late nineteenth century. Since then, the filmmaker has become an intimate of Vladimir Putin, and it was certainly through his influence that Putin began to read Ilyin. For Nikolay Mitrokhin, a specialist in Russian nationalism at the University of Bremen's Research Centre for East European Studies, 'Putin's personal interest in Ilyin, thanks to Mikhalkov, is incontestable.'[4]

Since perestroika, pre-revolutionary Russia and the elites who emigrated after the revolution have been in fashion, and Putin has not escaped this vogue. As a son of St Petersburg, he feels a certain fascination towards the intellectuals, military men and politicians who left the imperial capital for exile. 'The best of us', those who had helped Russian art and thought flourish in Paris, Berlin, Prague or New York, often in very difficult situations of exile, were endlessly celebrated in television series of the 1990s and 2000s. It was cheap and easy to revel in the myth of a 'true Russia' that had remained pure. It was pretended that émigrés would be reunited with the assets they had left behind, and some were welcomed ostentatiously to the Kremlin, especially those who proved themselves amenable to the federal regime. With his Russia Culture Fund, Mikhalkov selected the most reactionary Russian émigrés and instrumentalized them politically before 'offering' them to his friend Putin.

Ivan Ilyin specialized in Hegel, to whom he dedicated his doctoral thesis, 'The Philosophy of Hegel as a

Doctrine of the Concreteness of God and Humanity'. He situated himself within the tradition of religious thought influenced by German idealism, which had been dynamic in Russia since the nineteenth century. He wrote, for example, that 'man communicates with the divine element of the world and enters into living contact with God at the very moment of spiritual experience.'[5] Ilyin was fiercely opposed to the revolution of October 1917 and was eventually expelled from Russia in 1922, along with scores of other intellectuals, on the 'philosophers' ship'.[6] He settled in Germany and there he published one of his most celebrated works, mixing Hegelian dialectic with a call to arms against Bolshevik Russia. With *Resistance to Evil by Force* (1925), Ilyin refuted the theory of non-violence popularized by Leo Tolstoy, seeking to demonstrate that it does not violate Christian ethics—which he embraced—to fight evil, with force if needs be. When all peaceful means of countering an external aggression have been exhausted, he believed, it is necessary to make use of the sword. And even in that act, Ilyin thought, there was a historical necessity:

> The whole history of humanity can be summarized by the fact that at different times and within diverse communities *the best died at the hands of the worst*. And this will continue as long as the best do not decide to counter the worst with a planned and organized resistance.[7]

A resistance like Putin's, for instance—against NATO, the democratic opposition, the Chechens, and certain oligarchs such as Boris Berezovsky, Vladimir Gusinsky or Mikhail Khodorkovsky.

This 'virile' morality, consisting of a justification of violence in the name of doing good, stirred up considerable controversy when it first appeared, seemingly legitimizing state violence. Another philosopher, Nikolai Berdyaev, discerned the authoritarian, even totalitarian seeds germinating within this ethic, developed by a thinker who saw himself as anti-communist. 'Ilyin has been infected by the poison of Bolshevism,' he wrote. 'In its essence, the Bolsheviks could quite fully accept the book of I. Ilyin ... The Bolsheviks are conscious of themselves as the bearers of an absolute good and in the name of it they oppose by force whatever they regard as evil.'[8]

It is understandable that Ilyin's ardently anti-Soviet philosophy might have attracted the post-communist elites; according to Berdyaev, they shared the same value system. In 1933, when the Nazis took power in Germany, Ilyin published what he believed was a balanced article on 'the new national-socialist spirit'. At the end of his analysis, which systematically minimized the persecution of Jews, he identified in Nazism several positive traits:

> Patriotism; faith in the identity of the German people and in the strength of German genius; a sense of honour; readiness for self-sacrifice; discipline; social justice; trans-class, fraternal and national unity. This spirit is the basis of this entire movement's substance. It burns

> in the heart of every sincere Nazi, flexes his muscles, resounds in his words and shines in his eyes. One only has to see those believing faces, believing, to see that discipline, in order to understand the meaning of what is happening and to ask oneself: 'Does a people exist on the planet who would refuse to create for itself a movement of these dimensions and this spirit?' In a word, this spirit aligns German national socialism with Italian fascism. And not only that, but also with the spirit of the White Russian movement.[9]

Such sympathies, although ephemeral, were carefully erased from the Russian films about Ilyin between 2000 and 2010. It is true that Ilyin soon parted company with the Nazis when they asked for his help in rallying Russian émigrés to Hitler's ideology. He refused, found himself removed from his teaching posts, and emigrated to Switzerland in 1938. After the war, he listed the 'errors' of fascism and national socialism, including their anti-religious and anti-Christian nature, the creation of a totalitarian and one-party state, their extreme nationalism and despotism. Conversely, he paid tribute to Franco and Salazar, 'who have understood and are trying to avoid these errors. They do not call their regimes "fascist". Let us hope that Russian patriots will think through to the end the errors of fascism and national socialism, and will not repeat them.'[10]

For the Putin regime, then, in the words of historian Mitrokhin, 'Ilyin constitutes the Russian alternative to fascism',[11] a way of avoiding fascism while remaining close to it. Based in Switzerland until his death, Ilyin remained very close to the most radically anti-Bolshevik 'Whites'. He provided an ideological basis for the Russian All-Military Union, founded by the 'White' General Pyotr Wrangel and dedicated to overthrowing Soviet power. Yet he was far from being, as Nikita Mikhalkov claimed in his film devoted to Ilyin, 'the most famous Russian philosopher'.[12] His work is much less discussed and translated than that of Shestov, Berdyaev or Sergei Bulgakov, to mention only a few other thinkers who emigrated at the same time. Moreover, in post-Soviet Russia he is best known not for his works on Hegel, religion or art, but for his opinion pieces—articles written between 1948 and 1954 and collected in a thematic text on the future of Russia entitled *Our Mission*. It was the two volumes of this text, republished in 1993, that would later find their way onto the bedside tables of Putin's officials.

After several key speeches by the president, these unfortunates have felt obliged to read and then quote 'the great philosopher' at every turn. On 25 April 2005, during his formal address to the Federal Assembly, presenting a presidential report and the legislative programme for the coming months to representatives of both Chambers (the Duma and the Federation Council), Putin quoted Ilyin. But this first reference to the philosopher was a subtle one. In a passage on the building of an efficient political and judicial system to guarantee the country's development and democracy, he called on his government and the representatives present not to abuse their power, but to do everything possible to 'build up the institutions of a genuine democracy'.[13] Though this term, juxtaposed with 'formal democracy', springs as much from Marxist orthodoxy as from Ilyin's thinking, we should note that several months later, in September, a 'Civic Chamber' would be created, composed of civil society figures, in order to promote this 'genuine democracy'.

It was at this stage in his speech that the president cited Ilyin: '"State power", wrote the great Russian philosopher Ivan Ilyin, "has its own limits";[14] for it is "authority that reaches people from outside"'.[15] Elaborating with a lengthy citation, Putin joined Ilyin in arguing that 'scientific, religious and artistic creation'[16] should not be regulated, and that there should be no state interference in daily life.

This first extensive referencing of Ilyin sounds like a nod to the dictatorship of law and to the power vertical, notions promoted by Putin since his accession to the presidency. Power, because it comes from the people, must, we recall, respect the people and not provoke their reaction through coercion. But one can acquire a better understanding of Ilyin's thinking by reading an entire chapter of *Our Mission*'s first volume. 'The Principal Task of a Future Russia' is a programmatic text on what would happen to the country after the fall of communism and what should be done to escape chaos. 'We do not know when or how the communist revolution in Russia will meet its end,' admitted Ilyin.

> But we do know what will be the principal task of Russian national salvation and reconstruction: the rise to the top of the best—men devoted to Russia, who have a feeling for their nation, who contemplate their state, who are resolute, creative, offering the people not vengeance and decline, but the spirit of liberation, justice and unity between all classes. If the selection of these new Russian men is successful and takes place quickly, then Russia will rise up and be reborn in the space of several years. If that is not the case, Russia will fall from revolutionary chaos into a long period of post-revolutionary demoralization, decline and dependence on outside forces.[17]

One can imagine the astonishment that must have gripped Putin when Nikita Mikhalkov showed him these lines. This was more than a political programme: it was a portrait awaiting completion. A little further on in the chapter, Ilyin calls for the construction of a new 'Russian idea'. This cannot be 'the idea of "the people", of "democracy", of "socialism", of "imperialism", of "totalitarianism" ... A new idea is needed, religious in its sources and national in its spiritual meaning. Such an idea alone will be lead to the rebirth and re-foundation of tomorrow's Russia.'[18] In citing a relatively anodyne sentence from this text, Putin clearly intended to push all Russian leaders and officials to read this as an indirect description of himself and his future actions. Back in 2005, this wasn't a matter of structured philosophy, but more of a prophetic and flattering inspiration.

A year later, Putin hammered home this point in similarly solemn circumstances. This time, he used his annual speech to the Federal Assembly to point to another aspect of Ilyin's thought. Insisting that the army is part of society and the nation, he proclaimed:

> Reflecting on the basic principles on which the Russian state should be built, the well-known Russian thinker Ivan Ilyin said that the calling of soldier is a high and honourable title, and that the soldier 'represents the national unity of the people, the will of the Russian state, strength and honour'.[19]

With this in mind, the president emphasized, the country 'must always be ready to repel potential aggression from outside'.[20] Several years later, Putin again quoted Ilyin, the official ideologue of the White Army, at a ceremony in honour of military academy graduates, declaring: 'As the celebrated philosopher Ivan Ilyin said, "The Russian army will never forget the traditions of Suvarov, affirming that a soldier is also an individual."'[21] This quotation may simply have been incidental to the moment, but it nonetheless hints at Putin's ambition to restore Russian military might by rooting it in the history of the Russian Empire.

* * *

The context of Ilyin's time needs examining for it to be clear that he offered a coherent theory of the exercise of power, of the political regime best suited to Russia, and of the nation's political and historic role in the world. A visceral anti-communist, Ilyin was nonetheless no admirer of Western democracy. He refused to choose between 'totalitarianism, whether of the left, the right or the centre' and 'the way of Western European democracy'—that of 'formal democracy'. He dreamed of a 'democratic dictatorship', not one based on arithmetic but rather a 'democracy of quality, responsibility and service'.[22] He imagined what would happen when communist power crumbled, and announced that after a 'chaos that will last several years',[23] one of violence and 'separatist attempts backed by foreign powers', salvation would come in the form of 'national dictatorship'. Elections would not play an important role, and instead Ilyin hoped for a 'Guide', who 'will know what has to be done'. He concluded: 'This guide does not build a career, but serves; does not simply go through the motions, but truly fights; does not utter empty words, but strikes at the enemy; does not sell out to foreigners, but leads [his country].'[24] And so the 'Putinian' programme is written—and from it flows the model of the 'power vertical', of 'sovereign democracy' and hostility towards foreign powers (a theme shared with the Soviet past).

What of Ilyin's doctrine on Russia's relations with the rest of the world? The title of Putin's favourite Ilyin text[25] is categorical: 'What Dismemberment of Russia Entails for the World'.[26] If he has indeed reflected on this article, a mixture of Ilyin's Hegelianism, militarism and imperial nationalism, then Putin can't have entered into his Ukrainian adventure blindly or unprepared. From a typically post-Hegelian perspective, Ilyin claimed that Russia is not an 'artificially arranged mechanism', but 'an organism shaped by history and justified by culture'. It would thus be impossible to dismember it without causing it suffering, or even death. 'Imperialist neighbours', in a struggle also clearly Hegelian, would more or less overtly seek to seize territories such as Ukraine, the Baltic States, the Caucasus and Central Asia that were under natural Russian control. 'Russia would be transformed into a gigantic "Balkans", into an eternal source of wars.'

Why would the world wish to attack Russia? Because 'the peoples of the West neither understand nor tolerate Russian originality'. Their objective is thus to 'dismember Russia in order to force it under Western control, to dismantle it and finally to make it disappear'.[27] Their method, Ilyin believed, consists of the hypocritical championing of values such as 'freedom'.[28] Certain 'tribes', he maintained, were unfit to become states and should remain under the tutelage of neighbouring states; he listed the Flemish, the Walloons, the Croats, the Slovenes, the Slovaks, the Basques and the Catalans. But he was really thinking of the peoples who made up the

Russian Empire, and of Russia's Ukrainian, Caucasian and Asiatic 'little brothers'. Here again, the blueprint for the years to come had already been sketched out by Ilyin half a century before. Mikhalkhov had discovered it with amazement, and handed it over to Putin for its full realization.

4

THE CONSERVATIVE TURN

One month after his accession to the presidency, a student innocently asked Putin, 'The ageing of the soul leads to conservatism. What do you think?' The new president, whose virile and athletic image was in sharp contrast with the old and ailing Boris Yeltsin, responded, 'I wish to reassure you: I feel quite young. In any case, I don't feel my age.'[1] In other words, Putin wished to transform his country; he saw himself as a reformer and liberal, not a conservative. But, thirteen years later, when asked to comment on the statement 'Many people become conservative with age', he agreed: 'You're no doubt right. And yet I think it makes a certain amount of sense, because conservatism is by no means equivalent to stagnation. Conservatism means relying on traditional values, but in order to better work towards development.'[2]

What had happened in the intervening years? Putin may have wanted at the outset to project himself as a modernizer, but not without a certain rigidity. Presidential expressions that disconcerted democrats very quickly began to flourish: 'dictatorship of law', 'power vertical', the restoration of stability and Russian power. When compelled to justify these concepts to the German media in June 2000, he defended his vision of a 'strong state', which did not necessarily correspond to a 'dictatorship'. Playing to the 'Western ear', which he was already finding hypersensitive, Putin was willing to refer to an 'efficient state'.[3] To suppress, imprison and drive out the powerful businessmen of the 1990s, he invoked the 'threat of Russia's development in an oligarchic direction'.[4] At the end of 2002, he confirmed these maxims of his first term:

> People want stability. They don't want inertia and stagnation ... but they definitely want stability in the positive sense of that notion, they want to see light at the end of the tunnel, they want to live better, they want their children to have the prospect of a better life.[5]

He thus dismissed all 'political populism'[6] and claimed to be fitting his policies into a project of controlled reform.

Several months later, however, a new tone was emerging in some of Putin's statements. He declared at the Hermitage Museum in St Petersburg that 'culture is a very important vector of traditions, fashioning the Russian people in a united society and creating the foundation of the Russian state'.[7] Was he already showing his age? In any case, from this time onwards he would raise at every opportunity the idea of culture as the national bond holding together traditional values. He even began to add a moral sense to this apologia of culture and roots. While he continued to stress that 'the state must be modern', he also extolled 'holy Russia', 'the rebirth of traditions, the rebirth of the moral and ethical foundations of our culture, at the base of which, of course, lie Christian values'.[8]

This philosophy was crystallized following an event at the beginning of Putin's second presidential term (2004–8). The tragedy of Beslan unfolded on 1 September 2004, when Chechen separatist rebels took an entire school hostage on the first day of term in a small Russian Caucasian town. After a violent and chaotic operation by Russian special forces, 344 people, including 186 children, had lost their lives. Two weeks later, Putin announced that regional governors would henceforth no longer be elected but appointed, justifying this democratic regression by pointing to the alleged negligence of local officials.

At around the same time, Putin's utterances were becoming much more conservative in tone. Firstly, he considered that 'terrorists' brandishing 'religious slogans'[9] was primarily due to 'religious ignorance'. He called on religions to distance their adherents from extremism, and—seemingly forgetting that distorted religious instruction often leads to radicalization—decided to make the Russian Orthodox Church his ally in 'bringing morality' to the people. Indeed, his deep conviction, as he would admit several years later, was that 'only religion can provide the moral values without which humanity as a whole and we as individuals cannot live'.[10] Though he continued to emphasize, somewhat superficially, the multi-confessional nature of the Russian Federation, he was very openly counting on the powerful Orthodox Patriarchate of Moscow: 'Orthodoxy just happens to be the biggest of our religions. Almost 80 per cent of Russia's population feel that they have some connection with Orthodoxy.'[11]

Besides the trauma of Beslan, which convinced Putin to align himself with the Church and entrust it with the task of 'humanizing' the people, the president was shaken by the colour revolutions that came to destabilize his 'near abroad'.[12] In Georgia, at the end of 2003, the Rose Revolution brought to power the young pro-American Mikheil Saakashvili. A year later, the Orange Revolution in Ukraine swept aside the pro-Russian candidate Viktor Yanukovych in favour of the pro-Western reformer Viktor Yushchenko. Putin turned more resolutely to traditional values as he felt himself surrounded by hostile powers, with certain nations formerly part of the USSR having chosen to leave the Soviet universe and Russian patronage. In this choice Putin saw nothing more or less than a CIA operation. Not long after these events, Kremlin adviser Vladislav Surkov, with some help from political scientist and former Soviet dissident Gleb Pavlovsky, invented the notion of 'sovereign democracy' to underline the distinctions of Russia's approach to politics. As it was now sovereign, Russian democracy refused to march to the drum of Western democracies and, above all, would repel any interference in its affairs.[13]

Leaving this type of technocratic concept to his advisers, Putin then took up another theme that would mark the bedrock of his conservative trajectory: the establishment of demography as a national priority. This involved checking a decline in the birth rate that had potentially catastrophic national implications, and Putin sought to present this as not merely a social, but also a moral issue. At a meeting in August 2004 with the patriarch of Moscow, Alexy II, he proposed a plan to tackle 'the country's demographic problems, strengthening the family, ethical issues and questions surrounding the country's very high number of terminated pregnancies'.[14] What would emerge out of this vision was a gradual drift from defending family values towards open homophobia. Several years later, Putin was longer content with making allusions and established a direct link between natalist policy and the fight against homosexuality. Answering a question on Gay Pride, he declared: 'My relation to gay parades and sexual minorities in general is simple—it is connected with my official duties and the fact that one of the country's main problems is demographic. (Applause).'[15]

This was just the start. Another manifestation of the president's conservatism was to be seen in his relationship with new forms of technology. He has admitted that he does not use email.[16] He has criticized the Internet and the 'problems'[17] posed by the Web. In 2013, he deplored the decline of the book, due in his view to 'the rapid development of digital technologies', leading to a 'fall in the standard of general knowledge'.[18] Limiting Internet access is part of the president's intellectual platform.

The final aspect of the road towards conservatism during Putin's second term could be seen in 2007, with his defence of 'Russian cultural immunity' against foreign incursions. In the same year as the famous 'Munich speech', in which the president forcibly opposed the unipolar order advocated by the United States and its allies, a notable idea emerged: that culture should not only be accorded a moral and educative role, but also kept safe from foreign contagion. 'Of course, we must understand and accept the culture of other countries,' Putin conceded, before exclaiming, 'We must create the necessary conditions for the education of the young generation to take place in an atmosphere favourable to national culture', which would in turn encourage this generation's 'spiritual maturity'. As in the Soviet era, then, culture was becoming the armed wing of national policy.

* * *

Vladimir Putin's return to power in May 2012, after the Medvedev interlude, took place amidst a wave of increasingly overt conservatism. For several months, demonstrations unprecedented since the time of the USSR's collapse had shaken Russia. Citizens were protesting against the rigged legislative elections of December 2011 and against Putin's scheduled return to the presidency. His speeches were sounding more muscular than ever; on the bicentenary of the 1812 Battle of Borodino against French forces, he trumpeted his patriotism: 'We Russians must never forget our own land, its development and its future.'[19] His tone growing increasingly martial, he likened those protesting his return to supporters of Russia's defeat: 'National treachery!' He then exalted Orthodoxy's 'special part in our country's history'[20] since the baptism of Russia by Prince Vladimir, who rallied the Russian tribes around a unified state.

This fit of patriotism was nothing compared with what followed. Several weeks later, in mid-September 2012, Putin mounted a fresh charge on the issue of 'our young people's patriotic education', 'the values and moral foundations on which we can and must build our lives, educate our children, develop society, and, ultimately, strengthen our country'. The demographic future of Russia depended on such education, he argued, moving on to the 'fierce competition' between different 'value codes'. He denounced what he called 'well-orchestrated propaganda attacks'. 'These are not irrational fears, not my imagination, that is exactly how it really is,' he was at pains to point out: 'Attempts to influence the worldviews of entire ethnic groups, the desire to subject them to one's will, to force one's system of values and beliefs upon them is an absolute reality…' He denounced an '"every man for himself" mentality, intolerance and egotism—all of which he identified with the West. He appealed for patriotism, religion and military organization, before finally reaching his personal obsessions: 'In the modern world, children do not just learn in school. The moral and ethical climate of our society overall depends greatly on what they see, hear and read.' Attacking the Internet, his aim, he said, was to 'protect children from pornography, propaganda of violence, cruelty, amoral and indecent behaviour'.[21]

How to explain this sudden outburst of anger against Western culture, and what well-orchestrated attack was Putin referring to? In France in the same period, a pledge made by the new president, François Hollande—to enable same-sex marriage—was on the way to being realized, while in June 2013 a similar law was introduced in England and Wales. In Russia, meanwhile, mere weeks after this speech from Putin, the Duma announced that it would debate a new law against 'homosexual propaganda', to be voted on in January 2013 and became law that June. Here, Putin had found a hobby-horse behind which he could unite all of conservative Europe: the fight against 'homosexual culture'. The year 2012, in which Putin had retaken power, closed with a solemn warning delivered in his annual address to the Federal

Assembly: 'I would like all of us to understand clearly that the coming years will be decisive and perhaps even ground-breaking not only for us, but for the entire world as it enters a period of transition and possibly even shocks.'[22] Everything was now in place for the great conservative turn and the beginning of the offensive against the West.

What Russian analysts and journalists have called the conservative turn, and which had been in preparation for years, took shape in the autumn of 2013. Speaking before international specialists in Russia at the prestigious Valdai Club, Putin launched into a long and stupefying anti-modern and anti-Western diatribe. All the themes that he had been introducing one by one since 2000 now solidified around a defence of Russian national identity—made up of patriotism, Christian values, protection of the traditional family—against attacks from abroad 'in a rapidly changing world'.

He began by dismissing three options for building twenty-first-century Russia: nostalgia for 'Soviet ideology', which 'could not be brought back', a form of 'fundamental conservatism' that 'idealise[d] pre-1917 Russia', and finally 'an extreme, Western-style liberalism'. If 'a new national idea does not simply appear, nor ... develop according to market rules', if 'primitive ... attempts to civilize Russia from abroad [hadn't been] accepted by an absolute majority of our people', then the time had come, said Putin, to formulate a doctrine emerging from society as a whole, not one imposed from above.

It was at this point in his speech that Putin voiced his strongest attack yet on what he viewed as 'the many Euro-Atlantic countries ... that are actually rejecting their roots, including the Christian values that constitute the basis of Western civilization'. According to Putin, these nations were

> denying moral principles and all traditional identities: national, cultural, religious and even sexual. They are implementing policies that equate large families with same-sex partnerships, belief in God with belief in Satan. The excesses of political correctness have reached the point where people are seriously talking about registering political parties whose aim is to promote paedophilia. People in many European countries are embarrassed or afraid to talk about their religious affiliations.

This could only lead, he concluded, to 'a profound demographic and moral crisis'.[23]

Not long after this speech, Putin's press secretary was to claim that the Russian president had received reliable information 'from ministries and state departments, from the media and sociological researchers, from news agencies' and also from 'his friends, acquaintances and colleagues'[24] concerning this supposed paedophile political party. (The most likely of these is sources is the latter; we have some idea of what Putin, Yakunin and others close to the president talk about in private.) In public, Putin concluded that Russia would not accept a role as 'vassal' in this 'unipolar world'.[25] He also alluded in media interviews at this time to his 'conservative perspective'.[26]

Following his re-election, Putin repressed opponents, described NGOs benefiting from international funding as 'foreign agents', limited the right to protest and freedom of expression, forbade the adoption of Russian children by American citizens and banned 'homosexual propaganda'. On 12 December 2013, the twentieth anniversary of the post-Soviet Constitution of 1993, he summarized his ideas in a major speech to all the country's representatives. It was not by chance that this ideological offensive took place at the very moment when the Euromaidan protesters in Kiev were challenging the pro-Russian regime of Viktor Yanukovych. In yet another anti-Western outburst, Putin declared:

> Today, many nations are revising their moral values and ethical norms, eroding ethnic traditions and differences between peoples and cultures. Society is now required not only to recognise everyone's right to ... freedom of consciousness, political views and privacy, but also to accept without question the equality of good and evil, strange as it seems—concepts that are opposite in meaning.[27]

Claiming to embody the struggle against such moral equivalence, he called for the 'defence of traditional values' and admitted, 'Yes, of course, it's a conservative position.' The Russian press was by now celebrating 'Vladimir Putin's enlightened conservatism [which] guarantees him global leadership'[28] and quoted the rankings, like that of *Forbes* in October 2013, which placed Putin as the most influential man in the world. As for Russia's citizens, an opinion poll found that 56 per cent believed conservatism helped the country to safeguard traditions while allowing it to develop.

* * *

Which thinkers inspired this conservative turn? A website that appeared in 2014, Russian Idea, presented itself as the productive hub of such 'conservative political thought'. Historians of philosophy were active online, explaining the ins and outs of the 'conservative renewal' in Crimea in August 2014. The most influential among them had studied or taught at Moscow State University's philosophy faculty; this was the case with Boris Mezhuev, co-founder of the website. Born to a philosopher father in 1970, Mezhuev, like his entire generation, had rediscovered the Russian thinkers banned by the Soviet regime, notably Orthodox intellectuals opposed to the revolutionary camp. An expert on the best-known of these, Vladimir Solovyov, Mezhuev has since sought to serve as the ideologue of what he calls a 'conservative renaissance'. At that time he had an excellent outlet for spreading his ideas, as he was deputy editor-in-chief of the daily *Izvestia*, close to the centre of power.

Mezhuev made me a list of the Russian thinkers he believes have inspired the new ideological shift, including Konstantin Leontiev. On his website, Mezhuev describes the fathers of Putinian conservatism:

> We can count Leontiev, alongside Nikolay Danilevsky and Konstantin Pobedonostsev [a statesman and ideologue during the reign of Alexander III] as the 'triad' of the most outstanding representatives of conservative thought in nineteenth-century Russia ... From the new start of the 1980s and 1990s began Leontiev's true 'renaissance' ... Interest in his work has not diminished since ... The relevance of his ideas to current events simply must be stated.[29]

According to Mezhuev, Leontiev's philosophy is pertinent today because it 'consists of deploring Europe's chosen path of secularization while turning its back on its Christian roots—not to mention his hatred of democracy, which is currently very strongly felt in certain Russian milieus.'[30]

Leontiev was an unusual character. Nicknamed the 'Russian Nietzsche', he was born in 1831 into a noble family and liked nothing more than adventure. In 1854, he took part in the Crimean War as a doctor—which earned him at least some of the popularity he enjoys today in circles of power. He was an aesthete, a lover of heroic and archaic forms of beauty, as well as a mystic. After a long period spent on Mount Athos, this nineteenth-century Don Juan dreamed of becoming a monk, and secretly took vows in his later years at the Optina monastery, the setting for much of Dostoevsky's *The Brothers Karamazov*. He died in 1891 in another famous monastery, the Trinity Lavra of St Sergius in Sergiyev Posad, near Moscow. Paradoxically both sensual and mystical, despising bourgeois mediocrity and conformism, Leontiev left behind work that does not exhibit a brilliant system of philosophy, but is striking in its radicalism. He was, for example, disdainful of Dostoevsky's Christianity, a 'sugary syrup' too humanitarian for his tastes. Conversely, he glorified the severe and hierarchical customs of the Byzantine Church, eschewing any moralization of Christianity. His aristocratic outlook, his pessimism and his fondness for paradox made him almost a natural enemy of democracy, freedom, equality, secularization, comfort and eudaemonism—the idea that personal wellbeing should be pursued above all else. What must also have impressed readers close to Vladimir Putin was Leontiev's prophecy of a 'federal Europe' threatening to swallow up Russia and rob it of all its specificity. In one of his major works, 'Byzantinism and Slavdom', published in 1875, he announced: 'France, Germany, Italy, Spain, etc. ... will become regions of a new State. ... I will be told: "But that will never happen!" I will reply: Happy the man who believes that."'[31] In another essay evocatively entitled 'The Average European as an Ideal and Instrument of Universal Destruction', he warned: 'The Russians must fear it, must be terrified, so that history does not seduce us and lead us down this anti-cultural and ignoble path.' On the contrary, 'we must strive in every sense to strengthen our interior discipline'.[32]

This hatred of modern Europe did not prevent Leontiev from admiring the forms of Western medieval and Renaissance culture that he judged to be elevated and sublime. But he invented—or rather adapted to his predilection—a naturalist theory of the three ages of civilization. According to this theory, every civilization first lives through a period of original simplicity, then experiences its apogee in an era of 'blossoming complexity', before withering away in an age of resimplification and confusion. Europe, he believed, had been in a state of decadence since the Renaissance, no longer producing saints and geniuses but engineers, members of parliament and teachers of morality. It was uniform, both in its development model and its conformism, but at the same time disordered. Its inhabitants were lost souls, running in all directions to give meaning to their lives while incapable of recognizing any inspirational higher principle.

One can imagine how accurate this picture of Europe must have appeared to Putin and his circle, who were fighting against a model of the Western world that they thought threateningly homogenizing, at the same time as deploring its chaotic individualism and lack of grand designs or capacity for mobilization. Russia, by contrast, was placed by Leontiev in the ascendant phase of civilization. This is exactly what Putin meant when he quoted Leontiev in his conservative speech of September 2013: 'Russia—as the philosopher Konstantin Leontiev vividly put it—has always evolved in "blossoming complexity" as a state-civilization, reinforced by the Russian people, Russian language, Russian culture, the Russian Orthodox Church and the country's other traditional religions.'[33] In other words, Russia is complex because it is home to very diverse peoples and faiths, but is blossoming because these differences are in harmony, in a unique culture embodied and led by the state. Thus it was through a mobilization by and for the state that diversity would become unity—unity of culture and of destiny.

* * *

Leontiev is viewed as a predecessor of Oswald Spengler (1880–1936), author of *The Decline of the West* (1918–22). Opposed to the Enlightenment vision of uninterrupted progress that had been adopted in the eighteenth century, Spengler inspired those at the end of the First World War who believed that one world was coming to an end as another was born—and sometimes believed in the possibility of a civilizational convulsion. More generally, the new Putinian ideology has its origins not only in Russian philosophy but also in several Western variants of conservative thought, and especially in what has been called the conservative revolution in Germany between 1918 and 1933.

Nikolai Plotnikov, a historian of Russian and Germany philosophy at the University of Bochum in Germany, confirms that 'all the conservative thinking of the Weimar Republic is still in use today, notably Carl Schmitt, Ernst Jünger and even Ernst Niekisch, the theoretician of national bolshevism. All these authors have met with great success in Russian bookshops since the 2000s.'[34] It should be kept in mind that Ernst Jünger (1895–1998), involved in both world wars but hostile to Nazism, eulogized the spiritual and aesthetic dimensions of war.

Carl Schmitt (1888–1985), himself deeply committed to the Third Reich, created or revived several concepts that influence current Russian ideology. We can see in Putin's hostility towards humanitarian intervention the central idea of Schmitt's political theory, which held that nothing was more disastrous than a moral or judicial reading of politics. Just as law is guided by binary concepts of the just and the unjust, morality by concepts of good and evil, aesthetics by beauty and ugliness, so, Schmitt believed, politics possesses its own opposed guiding principles—friendship and enmity. In politics one has friends or enemies, nothing more or less; politics consists of either struggle or alliance between political bodies, but it is not to be judged through the exclusive prism of law or morality.[35] Heir presumptive and renovator of the Soviet dichotomy between 'ours' and 'yours', Putin has signed up to this notion of politics as an unadulterated balance of power. In his *Political Theology* (1922) or *Constitutional Theory* (1928), Schmitt promoted the concepts of acclamation and 'decisionism'—'sovereign is he who decides on the state of exception'. This must have been music to the ears of those of Putin's advisers who were searching for words to embody the conservative mobilization to underpin the new Russian politics.

But the Putinian turn, prepared over more than a decade, did not benefit from deep philosophical reflection, as with the birth of the US neo-conservative movement, whose roots go back at least to the 1960s. In Russia, this movement has borrowed from authors whose limitations have never really been challenged, but who have been instrumentalized to suggest the superiority of 'Russian civilization' over a West viewed as decadent. Vladimir Putin, strangely, seems above all obsessed by one question, that of homosexuality. This theme mixes together all of the very diverse elements that he had previously put forward: Christian values, loyalty to national history, patriotism, and distrust of the West. This third layer of Putinian ideology, superimposed over layers of both Sovietism and pseudo-liberalism, might be termed archaeo-conservatism.

5

THE RUSSIAN WAY

On 18 March 2014, in an address to the Russian Federation, Vladimir Putin made the most important speech of his life. It marked his first step as a head of state who would truly change the course of history. Essentially, Putin had been preparing for this moment for fifteen years. He had already had a few test runs, having forcibly detached from Georgia the separatist regions of South Ossetia and Abkhazia. But now he had crossed a decisive line: following the example of Ivan III and several other emperors, he had 'gathered together the Russian lands'. As an act of retaliation against the democratic Ukrainian revolution (which Russian officials termed a putsch by Kiev's supposed fascist junta), Putin had just sent unidentifiable Russian troops into Crimea and organized an improvised referendum there, before unexpectedly seizing the territory, which has belonged to Ukraine since 1954.

This was the first time since the Second World War that a European state had annexed a region that was part of another European state. This special operation was condemned by part of Crimea's population, notably the Tatars—the region's historic inhabitants, repressed and deported during the Soviet period—and challenged by both Ukraine and the rest of the world. Only Russia recognized the annexation. Given the extent to which it violated international law and broke the inter-state consensus that had guaranteed European stability since the end of Nazism, the act required justification. This was the aim of Putin's victory speech, made two days after the referendum and one day after the signing of the presidential decree formalizing Crimea's membership of the Russian Federation.

Putin tried to prove the profound 'Russianness' of the peninsula and the legality of the referendum, before coming to his central argument: the international community had denounced Russia for the annexation because the world disliked Russia and had always sought to isolate it, to prevent it from occupying the place it rightfully deserved. 'In short,' Putin declared,

> we have every reason to assume that the infamous policy of containment, led in the eighteenth, nineteenth and twentieth centuries, continues today. They are constantly trying to sweep us into a corner because we have an independent position, because we maintain it and because we call things [what] they are and do not engage in hypocrisy. But there is a limit to everything. And with Ukraine, our western partners have crossed

> the line, playing the bear and acting irresponsibly and unprofessionally.[1]

The meaning of these words was clear: Putin fully intended to defend Russia against a West that wished it harm. His country would henceforth claim, loud and clear, its right to follow its own path—a Russian way.

Before this moment, but especially since, Putin has exploited ad nauseam this idea that, throughout the ages, his country has been the victim of foreign interventions seeking to prevent Russia from 'being herself'. As president, he has harnessed the tools for a gradual counter-attack, played as an act of revenge for history. Following the interventions in Georgia (2008), Ukraine (2014) and Syria (2015), more recently he has deliberately established a system of clandestine intervention in electoral processes far from Russia's borders (see Chapter 9).

At the time of writing (November 2017), we don't yet know the final outcome of the ongoing US investigations into the links between Kremlin representatives and members of Donald Trump's presidential campaign. However, what we can say with certainty is that individuals sanctioned by the Russian regime intervened in the 2016 US presidential election campaign. For the Russian establishment—and the feeling was mutual—Trump's opponent Hillary Clinton was an absolute enemy, symbolizing the humiliation of the 1990s, when the collapse of the USSR led to NATO's intervention in Kosovo.

Donald Trump, on the other hand, was a figure who appealed to the Kremlin, despite his many misadventures: libidinous businessman, populist ideologue, economic isolationist, friendly idiot or even dangerous madman—all of these characters suited Putin just fine, and he sought to make Trump an ally, or at least a good foil. To this end, Clinton's emails were released online, and social media flooded with propaganda messaging designed to alter the course of the campaign. Such hybrid warfare—effective but never acknowledged by the perpetrating regime—has been present in Europe since 2014 and the events of that year in eastern Ukraine. Two years later, it has found another form in the United States.

Of course, on this occasion as before, President Putin has denied any Russian involvement: 'there is no basis to think that Russia interfered in the election process.'[2] But this hybrid cyber warfare, helped by Russia's IT expertise and the long Soviet tradition of influence and destabilization, is now cropping up all over the place: in 2017 alone, the Russian press painted the then French presidential candidate Emmanuel Macron as the victim of a sexual predator (his wife Brigitte, who is older than him), backed Angela Merkel's electoral opponents and gave support to the Catalan secessionists agitating for independence following the unauthorized October referendum.

In terms of ideology, while Steve Bannon, an agitator close to the far right, was Trump's chief strategist

(January–August 2017), the neo-Eurasian prophet Alexander Dugin appeared as a common reference-point between certain Russian and American presidential advisers.[3] One leader of the American 'alt-right', Richard B. Spencer, contributed to the publication of certain Dugin texts, translated by his wife, Nina Kouprianova. In short, far-right Eurasianism has apparently formed a bridge between Putin's Russia and Trump's America. But, more generally, when it comes to Putin's 'Russian way' it seems that any form of opposition to Western democracy is a welcome help—from populism and separatism to proto-fascism.

* * *

The theory of the Russian way, like Putinian conservatism, was slow to mature. The idea had its roots in the early days of Putinism, but only in a broad form. Among the primary ambitions of the young president, as he stated two days before being elected in March 2000, was the desire to 'give the country back its prestige and its major world role'.[4] After the humiliation of the end of empire, and a decade of post-Soviet democracy in which people lived through a quasi-permanent social and economic crisis, status had to be returned to Russia, and Putin wasted no time in calling on national and Orthodox values for help. The 'spiritual renaissance of Russia' for which he aimed was still to be in a context of 'the right to freedom for man and the citizen',[5] but his increasingly uninhibited allusions to 'holy Russia' revealed the 'particular role' that 'Russia has agreed to assume as the guardian of authentic Christian values'.[6] Putin accorded special value to the holy sites of Russian Orthodoxy and interpreted Christianity in the sense of a specific national identity, destined to play a part in world affairs. Elsewhere he sometimes referred to the 'philosophy of religion', which he judged 'very, very important',[7] as it had the potential to replace the communist ideology of old.

The desire for a role in international relations worthy of Russian power, married to the conviction that the country possesses a specific culture that could become universal, gradually created a belief that other states were intent on forcing the disappearance of this Russian particularity. Putin was hardly tempted by cultural globalization: 'I would not like my country, Russia, to lose its originality and its identity. I would like the cultural roots, the spiritual roots of Russia, of which we are so proud and so fond, and which shape us as individuals, to be preserved.'[8] For the time being, Putin was only opposing a global process that he thought encouraged uniformity, but soon, during the 2004 Ukrainian revolution that consecrated pro-European President Yushchenko's victory, he would allege that efforts had been made to 'isolate the Russian Federation'.[9] Putin's argument was as follows: because Russia refused to submit to the orders of a unipolar and homogenizing world, because it was determined to safeguard its specific Russian way, it was being prevented from influencing its neighbours, pushed into an impasse, isolated and marginalized. Russia henceforth had to defend its will to follow 'a path that is its own'[10] and to demand the right for this difference to be heard and respected.

Accusations became clearer over the years; Russia was to be tamed or spurned, not only because it was different but also because it was among the world's most powerful states. The United States was subduing many countries and marginalizing others in the name of human rights or by economic and military means. By 2007, Putin had ceased to mince his words: 'Frankly speaking, there are not so many countries in the world today that have the good fortune to be able to call themselves sovereign. You can count them on your fingers: China, India, Russia and a few other countries. All other countries are largely dependent, either on each other or on bloc leaders.'[11]

So, what are the main characteristics of this 'Russian originality'? Beyond Christian foundations, patriotism, attachment to tradition, and tolerance in a multi-ethnic space, Russia, it seems, also has its own version of democracy. Offended by 'attempts to use the lexicon of democracy to influence our domestic and foreign policy',[12] Putin has demanded the prerogative to reinterpret in his own way the notions of human rights or freedom of expression. He may have accepted the universality of democratic principles, but the same does not go for their terminology or concrete political expressions: 'Russia's democracy means the power of the Russian people with their own traditions of self-rule and not the fulfilment of standards imposed on us from the outside.'[13] In other words, the proclamation of a Russian way involves an adaptation of democracy to national political history, linked to forms of local direct democracy. Yet the reality is far from an apologia of the old traditions of Russia's north, judging by the abolition of elected governors in 2004. To Putin's mind, his country has even fewer democratic lessons to learn for having played such an essential role in world history: one shouldn't be a fastidious stickler for etiquette with a country that has saved one's life. According to him, 'it was precisely the strength of authentic, historic Russia, the Russia of Minin and Pozharsky, of Dmitry Donskoy and Alexander Nevsky, of Sergius of Radonezh and Seraphim of Sarov, that vanquished Nazism and saved the world.'[14]

This way of interpreting the Red Army's victory over Hitler is significant, but it is not new in terms of the philosophy of the Russian way. It looks back to the popular fervour that repulsed the Napoleonic armies in 1812, and it recalls the struggles for national independence against the Poles and the Lithuanians, the Tatars and the Teutonic Knights. It revives the myth of a people united against a foreign aggressor. It subsumes an entire theory of the national-popular principle (in Russian, *narod* means both 'nation' and 'people'), a theory widely developed in the Slavophile tradition, as we shall see.

'At all the most critical moments in our history,' Putin has said, 'our people look to their roots, to their moral foundations and religious values.'[15] In this 2013 interview, he went on to quote Stalin addressing his people as 'brothers and sisters' and not as 'comrades', appealing to a more profound identity than that defined by Soviet citizenship. In other words, the notion of the 'Russian way' bases the nation's politics on certain qualities attributed to the Russian people, qualities that may have been slowly sculpted by the country's Orthodox culture. But what are they? Putin listed some of them in his 2012 annual address to the Federal Assembly, lamenting that they were not more prevalent: 'charity, empathy, compassion, support and mutual assistance'.[16] These are the values traditionally attributed to the Russian version of Eastern Christianity by numerous writers, theologians and philosophers. The instrumentalization of the Christian religion has never been so forceful.

Putin has gained a heavyweight ally in one of the twentieth century's most celebrated Russians, the writer and dissident Alexander Solzhenitsyn. The author of *The Gulag Archipelago*, exiled from 1974 in Switzerland and then the United States, moved back to Russia in 1994. Several months after Putin's accession to the presidency in 2000, Solzhenitsyn received him in his house near Moscow. Despite his misgivings when faced by the new president—a pure product of the Soviet regime, its *nomenklatura* and the political violence of the KGB—Solzhenitsyn was also a supporter of emphatic power and a special path for Russia. He did not want Russian democracy to become a mere clone of the Western model; he was fearful of Russia's 'encirclement' by NATO and alarmed by the future prospects of Russian speakers in the Central Asian republics. The two men conversed for more than two hours as Solzhenitsyn dispensed his advice on how to 'reorganize our Russia'.[17] Putin later remarked that he had followed this advice in terms of the self-management of local power,[18] but two years after their meeting, Solzhenitsyn was bitter: in an early 2002 interview with *Nouvelles de Moscou*, he complained, 'I certainly gave him good advice but he followed none of it'.[19]

Solzhenitsyn may have felt that his views on local democracy and his ecological concerns had been ignored, but that didn't stop Putin from feting his new friendship with the writer, whom he repeatedly quoted. He presented him with a national award in June 2007, stating: 'Millions of people associate the name and work of Alexander Isayevich Solzhenitsyn with Russia's fate.'[20]

The idea of a 'flesh and blood'[21] belonging to Russia forms the basis of Putinian patriotism. Solzhenitsyn's hostility towards the Enlightenment, condemning both socialism and liberalism, was perfectly suited to the Russian ideology that the president was in the process of developing, and so Putin incorporated the writer into his anti-Western discourse, using and abusing what he borrowed from him. In his 2006 address to the Federal Assembly, he quoted him on 'one of the most vital problems the country faces, the demographic problem, or, in A.I. Solzhenitsyn's happy expression ... the issue of "conserving the people" (Applause).'[22] After Solzhenitsyn's death in 2008, Putin signed a decree announcing an official national homage on the centenary of his birth in 2018.[23] The former anti-communist dissident had become an official figure of the new Russia, whose words would help to justify all imperialist adventures—especially in Ukraine.

* * *

Alexander Solzhenitsyn was the heir to a long Russian philosophical tradition, the Slavophile movement. Does Putin's affirmation of the specific nature of the 'Russian way' mean that he has appropriated it? Put very simply, since the beginning of the nineteenth century Russian thought has been divided into two great and opposite tendencies. On the one hand were the Westernizers, who believed that Russia's vocation from Peter the Great onwards was to be fully part of Europe and to catch up with it by abandoning imperial absolutism, restrictions on freedoms and the defence at all costs of its Orthodox identity and nationalism. One of the first representatives of this current was Piotr Chaadayev (1794–1856), who published his first 'Philosophical Letter' (in French) in the journal *Teleskop* to stupefaction and controversy. For Chaadayev, Europe enjoyed a 'hereditary patrimony of ideas', namely 'The ideas of duty, justice, law, order'.[24] Russia, by contrast, had missed every opportunity to participate in global culture:

> Alone in the world, we have given nothing to the world, we have taken nothing from the world; we have not poured a single idea into the mass of human ideas; we have contributed nothing to the progress of the human spirit, and anything that has reached us from that progress we have deformed.[25]

As for the great emperors who loved and travelled in the West, like Peter the Great or Alexander I, conqueror of Napoleon, no lineage could be traced from them: 'Once, a great man [Peter the Great] wanted to civilize us, and in order to give us a foretaste of enlightenment he threw us the mantle of civilization: we took up the mantle, but we didn't touch the civilization.'[26]

Chaadayev was declared insane by the authorities and banned from further publication. Whereas he was still a Christian thinker, other pro-Western theorists of his time grew apart from religious belief, some vehemently so. Alexander Herzen (1812–70), who clearly led this tendency, was influenced by French thought: by Saint-Simon, Fourier, Cabet, Louis Blanc and George Sand. An adversary of religion, he left Russia in 1847 to publish a journal in exile; he knew Proudhon, corresponded with Bakunin and campaigned in favour of socialism, revolution and materialism. The powerful critic Vissarion Belinsky (1811–48), an admirer of Hegel and Feuerbach, defended realism in art and considered himself a socialist and an atheist. This trend would gradually inspire the radical Russian youth described by Dostoevsky in *Demons*.

Against these Westernizers were the Slavophiles, who were also influenced by German philosophy, and especially by Hegel and Schelling. They wished to nurture a sense of national genius founded on a religious view of the world, on the virtues of the Russian people or the particularities of their social organization. The Slavophiles were often Muscovites attached to the traditions of that city of 'forty times forty' churches, and to the old customs of the nobility. Resistance to the Napoleonic invasion had, they thought, facilitated a national and popular uprising, and this surge had defeated the imperialist movement born of the abstract values that had emerged from the French Revolution. Alexei Khomiakov (1804–60), one of their leading lights, was a great hunter and a landed nobleman, yet close to the peasantry, whose emancipation he anticipated. In 1836, he responded to Chaadayev by publishing a letter of his own, addressed to a female friend: Chaadayev's article 'annoyed you', he claimed, 'and you repeat despite yourself: are we really so useless in comparison with Europe, do we really resemble children adopted by the common family of humanity?'[27]

For Khomiakov, the Westernizers erred in forgetting Russia's own riches: 'We have overlooked the work of improvement in everything that is ours, for we have been inspired with love and respect only for what is foreign to us'; 'We do not respect our mother tongue, our ancient simplicity of customs is often replaced by artifice.' His attack on the Westernizer movement was full-frontal: 'Why do they live like guests in their homeland? Why don't they speak in Russian, write in Russian, or even think in Russian?' Against a superficial and snobbish fascination with Europe, Khomiakov called on his contemporaries to discover the riches of Orthodox theology, the principle of collectivity that governed peasant life, and the qualities of the people.

The other founder of the Slavophile movement, Ivan Kireevsky (1806–56), also engaged in this debate. In 1838, he echoed Khomiakov: 'I have no intention of writing a satire of the West. Nobody knows better than me the price of the comfort of collective and individual life that [Western] rationalism produces.'[28] Yet he also lambasted what he called a 'state of moral apathy, absence of conviction, general egotism'; faults that 'cry out for new moral forces that do not originate in reason, a new vital energy that does not emerge from calculation.'[29] Attacking individualism, the dullness of abstraction, the mechanical routine of existence in the West, Kireevsky also celebrated the organic togetherness of Russian popular life, nourished by a vibrant Christian faith.

Other Slavophile thinkers like Konstantin Aksakov (1817–60) or Yuri Samarin (1819–76) gave further impetus to this movement in the nineteenth century. Though many philosophers have been able to enrich or transcend it, the dualism between Westernizers and Slavophiles has shaped the Russian intellectual domain since that time. This fault line survived the revolution of 1917 to persist even among the communist elites and within the party's Politburo, expressing itself in Soviet-era journals. Among the USSR's dissidents, a Westernizing Sakharov stood in contrast to the Slavophile Solzhenitsyn.

But is Putin a Slavophile? He has been known to quote Aksakov,[30] but it is hard to identify any real influence of the so-called first generation of Slavophiles on the Russian president. According to the philosopher Nikolai Plotnikov,

> many have wanted to see in Putin's politics a continuation of Slavophilia. The idea of a special [Russian] way is very prevalent among them, but it is intellectual, religious, and not at all political. There was no political imperialism among the first Slavophiles, at least until the Polish insurrection of 1861. The Slavophile vision was romantic, as in Germany in the same period. It contained a universalist element.[31]

Another Russian philosopher, Nikolai Berdyaev, who has written on Khomiakov, had already argued this: 'in Khomiakov, aversion to politics, or apoliticism, are

Russian national traits ... As with all the Slavophiles, Khomiakov saw the mission of the Russian people as lying not in political life but in the supreme existence of the mind.'[32] The Slavophile ideal, then, was organic and 'domestic',[33] and had little in common with the cold administration of a state.

'All the Slavophiles were opposed to the sovereignty of the state,' continued Berdyaev, 'they loathed bureaucracy; for them the tsar was a father and not a formal authority, and society was the organic unity of a free love.'[34] In essence, Slavophile doctrine could not be transformed into real politics and, above all, it justified no form of imperialism. According to the Slavophiles, the Russian people, agriculturalists par excellence, were gentle and peaceful, seeking primarily to cultivate their land and protect their village communities. In contrast, the notion of empire was, for Khomiakov for instance, deeply Western and, more specifically, Roman. Russians, in Slavophile eyes, were incapable of being aggressive conquerors or colonizers. This early Slavophile idealization of the people precluded any theoretical support for the conquest of new lands by the tsars.

Alexandre Koyré, also a historian of philosophy, has likewise shown that we cannot equate the first Slavophiles of the 1830s and 1840s with ultranationalists. He points out that 'they themselves had to feel internally foreign in Europe, and foreign in Russia, in order to both experience the aspiration to re-immerse themselves in the very sources of national life and to commune with "the people", and, simultaneously, to dream of a harmonious and complete civilization.'[35] Moreover, 'the most Westernized were not the Westernizers', since the Slavophiles, born into grand aristocratic families, had studied in Germany, while the Westernizers belonged to different social circles and were perhaps more rooted in Russian life.[36]

Ultimately, according to Nikolai Plotnikov, 'the central symbol of the "particular way" defined by the Slavophiles is the union of Church and state. But that idea doesn't work at all these days. One might have imagined such a union in the 2000s, when Vladimir Putin was relying heavily on the Orthodox Church, especially for his educational projects. Then, that alliance was very acceptable. But when, from 2014 onwards, we found ourselves faced with concrete political situations, as in Ukraine, the vacuity of this ideal became apparent. Political interests were even clashing with religious interests. Indeed, in Ukraine the majority of the people are Orthodox. The Russian Orthodox Church found itself between a rock and a hard place,'[37] he concluded, trying to both defend religious believers hostile to Moscow and avoid a quarrel with Putin.

* * *

Essentially, it is impossible to trace Putinian policy, which is statist, administrative and imperialist, back to

Slavophilia in its original form, which was far richer, more complex and freer—inherently irreducible to any state ideology. Rather, Putin's doctrine is much closer to that of another Russian philosopher, who is often classified as a 'second generation Slavophile'. Nikolay Danilevsky (1822–85) always advocated a form of Slavophilia oriented towards praxis—far from the purely cultural and 'dreamlike' visions of Khomiakov or Kireevsky. As Boris Mezhuev told me, today Danilevsky is the primary inspiration behind Putinian policy, since 'he has shown that the West is not universal'. Mezhuev even predicts a bright political future for Danilevsky, who is buried in Crimea, and whom he would like to see elevated to the rank of official thinker of the current national renewal. In his major work, *Russia and Europe* (1871), Danilevsky proposed a union of all Slavs under Russian leadership, a project, he said, motivated by the impossibility of his country becoming part of Europe. Russia was too original, too different to ally itself with the West, and another major obstacle was its size: 'It cannot be denied that Russia is too enormous and too powerful to be merely one of the great European powers.'[38] Moreover, when not exploiting it, Europe rejected Russia, within a structural relationship of mutual enmity. Only what Danilevsky called a Slavic Union could compete with a united Europe.

There was no need to fear general Russian domination. On the contrary, the union of all Slavs would allow a new global equilibrium, against any stray impulses of Western hegemony. And Russia had everything to gain from facing up to the West without weakness: 'Struggle with the West is the only salutary means of curing our Russian culture, as it is for advancing Pan-Slavist sympathy.'[39] Drawing on Hegel's affirmation in his *Elements of the Philosophy of Right* of 'the ethical moment in war'[40]—the effective union of the private citizen and the state, since each citizen is ready to sacrifice his worldly goods and even his own life for collective salvation—Danilevsky considered that popular mobilization in war represented a special process of fermentation in the evolution of a cultural and political renaissance. He even formulated a 'law of historical economy' whereby a reservoir of vital forces had been accumulating in Russia for centuries; part of the population, 'protected' by forests, steppes and mountains, had 'continued ... to develop silently, saving up future strength.'[41] This 'ethnographic tribal energy'[42] would one day find the means to expend itself.

When he referred to the interior strengths that Russia could marshal in the coming confrontation with the West, Danilevsky also explained that the 'ethical particularity' of the Russian people was its 'osmosis with its leader';[43] this created what he termed a 'disciplined enthusiasm,'[44] whereby governing institutions worked in perfect tandem with a total mobilization of popular forces. Danilevsky emphasized that the world had rarely, if ever, witnessed a strength of this nature, the Crusades having demonstrated a distinctly 'non-disciplined enthusiasm'. Europeans did not possess the heroism and unity that alone would enable them to beat the Russians and the progress of their historic mission.

In the last chapter of his work, Danilevsky rebuffed all those who did not believe in the specificity of Slavic culture, and attempted a little 'divination' to describe what that culture would look like after the eventual victory over Europe. The first and most important aspect of the 'Slavic cultural-historical type'[45] for Danilevsky was religion; he viewed Russians as a people chosen by God to preserve religious truth in the world. Another, related idea borrowed from the first-generation Slavophiles was that the people embodied such religiosity in their 'character'—aversion to violence, humility, respect and so on. Besides religion, Slavs could also be characterized by their capacity for political independence and their love of civil liberty. Yet for Danilevsky, Slavic civilization was only at its beginning—to fully realize itself, it had no choice but to stop its servile imitation of the West. And to achieve this goal, it had to fight the West.

Today, *Russia and Europe* serves as a gospel for the Russian political elite and within it lies part of the Putinian project. The idea of achieving the 'Russian way' through a confrontation with Western Europe has galvanized the Kremlin's advisers. Another salient characteristic of Danilevsky's doctrine should be mentioned: just like Leontiev and Lev Gumilev, another thinker cited by Vladimir Putin whom we shall discuss in due course, Danilevsky hid his expansionist aspirations behind scientific neutrality. Trained as a botanist, he viewed the history of civilizations like that of botanical or animal species—in a schema where states of conception, blossoming and decline succeed one another according to specific 'vital energies'. This claim to scientific status, as Berdyaev points out, radically separates the speculative philosophy of the first Slavophiles from Danilevsky's positivism. The latter 'supported the great mission of Russia with openly naturalist arguments; his Slavophilia was not validated religiously, but according to natural sciences—ethnographically, linguistically, by the doctrine of races and of types of evolution'.[46] Such philosophy with scientific pretensions is something that appeals to Vladimir Putin.

6

THE EURASIANIST DREAM

On 29 May 2014, Russia, Kazakhstan and Belarus solemnly signed a treaty of economic union. This was intended to be swiftly transformed into a Eurasian Economic Union, allowing the free movement of people, capital, goods and services. A single currency and citizenship had been mentioned, but these did not feature in the treaty's text. Nor did Kazakhstan and Belarus any longer seem quite so keen to accelerate integration—the mood was not one of enthusiasm. The great project of Vladimir Putin's third term had been impeded by events in Ukraine. First, the Russian president had envisaged such a structure to include Ukraine, but the latter had turned its back on Russia. Then Russia's war in Ukraine, in the name of defending Russian-speaking populations, had dampened relations with Moscow's Belarusian and Kazakh partners. This has not discouraged Putin from incorporating new members: Armenia joined the Union on 2 January 2015, and Kyrgyzstan on

29 May that year. But the Eurasian Union, which Putin wishes to make an equivalent of the European Union, is still in its infancy.

Even in the earliest days of his presidency, when he was playing the Westernizer, Putin did not fail to overlook the other side of Russia's geopolitical balancing act. Though he reaffirmed that 'Russia's culture and the traditions that are the basis of its development bond it to European civilization', he also pointed out that, 'of course, we are also in Asia',[1] which would point toward 'normal and friendly' relations with Central Asia, China, India and Japan. His early visits within this region were intended to confirm such relations. Yet it only took some months of already antagonistic interaction with Europe and the United States (over the enlargement of NATO, the controversy surrounding Putin's attitude to the sinking of the submarine *Kursk* in August 2000 and the irreverent tone of the American media) to make the Asian side of the equation seem the more attractive.

In an article entitled 'Russia: New Eastern Perspectives', President Putin affirmed that 'Russia has always felt itself to be a Eurasian country. We have never forgotten that the main part of the Russian territory is in Asia. Frankly, we have not always made good use of that advantage.'[2] But now it was time to reorient Russian policy in an easterly direction. In his third inaugural speech in May 2012, Putin emphasized the need for a new world stage for Russia:

> We have travelled a great and difficult road together, believing in ourselves and our strength and ability. We have strengthened our country and [restored] our dignity as a great nation. The world has seen a Russia risen anew ... We have everything we need today to continue our development and progress.

The aim of this progress was 'To become a leader and centre of gravity for the whole of Eurasia'. Practically nobody foresaw the events of the months ahead, but Putin warned: 'These coming years will be crucial for shaping Russia's future in the decades to come.'[3] The nature of this grand design was confirmed in his annual end-of-year address to the Assembly in 2013, when he described the development of Siberia and the Russian Far East as 'our national priority for the entire twenty-first century'.[4]

The first leader to develop the Eurasianist doctrine politically was certainly not Putin, but the Kazakh president Nursultan Nazarbayev (1991–), along with the heads of ex-Soviet states like Kyrgyzstan or Turkish-speaking territories within federal Russia such as Tatarstan, Buryatia and Kalmykia. In 1996, Nazarbayev created the L.N. Gumilev University, named after a twentieth-century Eurasianist. Putin was happy to give Nazarbayev the credit for this idea: 'of course, this came from you,' he congratulated him.[5] Speaking to the young Russians of the 2014 Seliger Forum, his modesty went further: 'The Eurasian Union, I have to admit it wasn't me who came up with the idea.' But on this occasion he forgot Nazarbayev, instead looking back to Russian thinkers: 'Philosophers know where this idea of a Eurasian Union came from and how it developed, who supported it in Russia. Then the Kazakhs picked it up...'[6]

* * *

As Putin says, the Eurasian project has its origins in philosophy. Defeat in the Crimean War in 1856, against France, Britain and the Ottoman Empire, produced a certain disillusionment with Europe, and Russia began to turn towards Asia.[7] But the Eurasianist current really took shape in the 1920s after the Russian Revolution, among émigré thinkers in Prague, Sofia, Vienna, Berlin and Paris. One of its representatives, Pyotr Savitsky (1895–1968), refuted the Europe-Asia divide symbolized by the Urals, instead proposing the existence of a 'third continent', a 'geographical world apart':[8] Eurasia, whose centre was Russia. This entity had a certain ecological coherence, as it brought together, from east to west, tundra, taiga, steppe and desert, while three plains wove it together from north to south.[9] Its homogeneity was also clear from the point of view of geographical relief (almost non-existent if one overlooks the 'false frontier' of the Urals) and climate, giving rise to the notion of a unified territory.

This continent, moreover, was not only different; it also gave geographical meaning to a large part of the world. 'Russia-Eurasia is the centre of the Old World,' wrote Savitsky.

> Take out this centre, and all its other parts, and that whole system of continental margins (Europe, the Near East, Iran, India, Indonesia, China, Japan) are transformed into a 'dispersed structure'. This world, situated to the east of Europe's frontiers and to the north of 'classical' Asia, is the link that forms them into a whole. This is evident today and will become even more so in the future.[10]

The linguist Nikolai Trubetzkoy (1890–1938) attempted to demonstrate that this region was home to a coherent grouping of languages, despite their differences. If a law explaining diversity of languages existed, he argued, then there must also have existed a meta-continent embodying this harmony of differences: Eurasia.

The Eurasianist movement diverged from others that we have already explored. Contrary to the Westernizers, the Eurasianists criticized the claim of 'Eurocentrism' to be the only force for progress in modern history. According to Trubetzkoy, 'we must accustom ourselves to the idea that the Romano-Germanic world, with all its culture, is our worst enemy. We must knock down and trample pitilessly underfoot the social ideals and preconceptions borrowed from the West, which always guide our intellectuals' ideas.'[11] But the Eurasianists also distinguished themselves from the Slavophiles, on one major point concerning Russian history. In Russia, the long period of Tatar-Mongol domination, which lasted from the thirteenth to the fifteenth century, was traditionally recalled as an age of terror, persecution and arbitrary rule, during which the Orthodox Russian people endured two centuries of foreign oppression. The Eurasianists re-evaluated this period, arguing that it had encouraged the union of the Russian princes. The Mongol presence, just like the Arab presence in Spain, also fostered an element of progress, while the Tatar hordes brought an enormous amount to Russia in terms of economic and financial competence, political management and military efficiency, as well as real religious tolerance.

Evoking the figure of Genghis Khan, Trubetzkoy wrote: 'He was not only a great conqueror, but was also a great organizer. Like all major statesmen, he did not merely command and administer according to narrowly practical conceptions of the present moment, but according to elevated principles and ideas linked to an ordered system.'[12] In other words, Eurasianism was a doctrine that fully integrated non-Russian, notably Turkish-speaking, peoples of the region. Islam was not viewed by most of its exponents as an enemy, indeed, quite the opposite. Finally, in contradistinction to Ilyin (see Chapter 3), many Eurasianists viewed favourably the revolution of 1917 and the birth of a geopolitical giant on the lands of Eurasia, since this marked Russia's break as a Eurasian power with a moribund European universe, the antithesis of Russia's eastern, or Turanian, identity.

* * *

The Eurasianist movement, driven underground during the Soviet era, was rediscovered in the 1990s and has since enjoyed immense popularity across the post-Soviet region. The most celebrated figure of its renewal, despite numerous misapprehensions, is Alexander Dugin,[13] who, with his prophet's beard and steely blue gaze, is sometimes thought of in the West as Putin's 'guru'. This is not the case—according to the former economic adviser Andrei Illarionov, 'Dugin's crass proclamations insult the president's intelligence' and it is highly unlikely that they see one another personally. But Putin must have been influenced, whether he likes it or not, by Dugin's fanatical media activities.

Concocting a strange mixture of Eurasianism and doctrines connected to the far right, Dugin is an unconditional supporter of Carl Schmitt and the creator of national bolshevism Ernst Niekisch; he is a disciple of both the anti-modern traditionalism of René Guénon and the fascist paganism of Julius Evola. He prides himself on his occultism, like the mysterious Romanian writer Jean Parvulesco (1929–2010), who was a former OAS activist,[14] a friend of certain New Wave filmmakers[15] and a Putin enthusiast. Dugin also considers himself heir to the Belgian revolutionary nationalist thinker

Jean Thiriart (1922–92) and, as a French-speaker, has long been very welcome among the French 'new right'; he often quotes Alain de Benoist. Some of Dugin's works have been translated into French, with prefaces by the anti-Semitic theorist of the 'Égalité et réconciliation' (Equality and Reconciliation) movement, Alain Soral. In one of these, written in 2009, Dugin advocates a fight against the liberal and democratic West in the name of the Eurasian empire, attempting to show that 'liberal globalization' is dragging us

> towards the abyss of virtuality's post-modernist dissolution. Our youth already has one foot in this abyss: the codes of global liberalism insinuate themselves with increasing efficiency at an unconscious level; in people's habits, in advertising, glamour, technologies, networking models. Loss of identity, not only national or cultural identity but also sexual and, soon, human identity, is now commonplace.[16]

Dugin amalgamates Eurasianism with the far right's theory of a 'new world order', adding to the blend some occultism and messianism—one chapter of this 2009 book is entitled 'Global democracy as the kingdom of the Antichrist'.[17] The great choice for Russia, he believes, is whether to submit to a debilitating globalization or instead to personify resistance. He has observed that before 2012, Putin was poised to 'wait and see': 'Those in power rejected direct Westernization, but nor did they adopt an alternative position (e.g. Slavophile,

Eurasianist). They remained frozen.'[18] But, he warned, 'it will not be possible to "stretch the elastic" beyond a certain critical point. Those in power will be forced to move toward a choice, one that will determine the future logic of relations with the West.'[19] In 2009, five years before the annexation of Crimea, he predicted a confrontation with the West over those post-Soviet states tempted to turn towards Europe and the United States. According to Dugin, 'if Georgia and Ukraine entered the ambit of the American empire ... Russia would see its imperial project blocked.'[20] Thus, 'the countdown to prevent the annexation of Ukraine by the Atlanticist empire has already begun.' After the 2008 'warning shot' of the invasion of Georgia, he wrote, Russia was ready to follow through. 'We cannot exclude having to fight a battle for Crimea and eastern Ukraine,'[21] he concluded.

I interviewed Dugin about the philosophers who inspire Putin. He believes that the president follows several layers of ideological model. 'First and foremost, Putin, with his Soviet education and KGB experience, is a *homo sovieticus*. In his view of the world, capitalism is an enemy. Onto this foundation he has added a layer of imperial Russian and conservative nationalism emanating from the émigré White Guard movement and especially Ivan Ilyin, who opposed the Eurasianists. But Ilyin is not an original thinker. He predicted nothing. From a philosophical point of view, he's a nonentity. Besides, Putin is not anti-communist like Ilyin was. Essentially, his championing of Ilyin only serves a technical, internal purpose: it is primitive thinking for primitive people', in other words the servants of those in power.

Dugin identifies a third layer to Putinian ideology, one he recognizes from his familiarity with the works of Parvulesco and the European projects of Jean Thiriart: 'Putin wants to create a union of European Christian realms' based on the model supposedly put forward by Russian philosopher Vladimir Solovyov. This union would involve a 'conservative utopia' through which the ancient European kingdoms, rediscovering their Christian identity, would unite 'under the strategic control of Russia', 'to fight against the Antichrist'. However, according to Dugin, the fourth ideological layer—Eurasianism—is more important. Indeed,

> this doctrine is not just one ideology among many. It springs from the Slavophile tradition, above all from the second-generation Slavophiles like Leontiev, Danilevsky or even Dostoevsky. But the Eurasianists were more coherent than the Slavophiles. They studied Russian civilization in a more logical and rational way. Above all, Eurasianism touched the deepest nerve in Russian history. It brought together what was common in the White and Red, the monarchical and socialist histories of the country.

Eurasianism also reconciles the different periods of Russian national history. 'Today, Eurasianism finds its full relevance in the growing confrontation between the

Atlanticist West and Eurasia,' says Dugin. According to him, Putin mixes all these ingredients, also throwing in 'realism on the international stage, which, for example, has allowed him to enlarge his zone of influence by opportunistically seizing Crimea'. Politically and strategically, 'Putin intends to build up a Eurasian empire' against American influence. 'Within three years,' Dugin predicted, 'he will take over the part of Ukraine that's on the right bank of the Dniepr.' As for western Ukraine, which would keep Kiev as capital, it 'could never embody a state'; its only possible function would be as 'a folkloric zone of Ukrainian identity' without any political independence.[22]

* * *

If Eurasianism is the most essential of the Putinian ideologies, what is the precise nature of Putin's inspiration? After all, he doesn't associate with Dugin, and certainly knows little about the Eurasianists of the past. On the other hand, he is very interested in a thinker often considered to be the missing link between the original doctrine of the 1920s and its current, more or less faithful, reinterpretations. This thinker is Lev Gumilev (1912–92), an unconventional character who is very well-known today across the whole post-Soviet region. The son of the poets Nikolai Gumilev and Anna Akhmatova, he lived a large part of his life in St Petersburg, Putin's birth town—when he was not in the Gulag. The political commentator Alexander Morozov claims that, according to reliable sources, Putin took part in a study circle on Gumilev's thought at the end of the 1990s: 'He has quite a deep knowledge of it'.[23] Indeed, Gumilev is practically the only Eurasianist that Putin quotes, and he speaks of him as if he knew him personally; in 2000, he told Gumilev's widow Natalia, 'In Russia we celebrate the memory of Lev Gumilev with a particular warmth.'[24]

In 2004, in the new Kazakh capital of Astana (home to the Gumilev Eurasian National University), Putin remarked that 'Gumilev's ideas have now reached the masses' and that Kazakhstan was trying 'to accomplish in the real world what this great Russian thinker [had] set out in the past'. Putin then claimed that one only had to unfold a map to understand that 'Russia lies in the centre of Eurasia'.[25] He also used Gumilev's Eurasianist rhetoric in the 2000s to win the goodwill of the powerful Republic of Tatarstan, which is part of the Russian Federation but was then showing signs of wanting autonomy. In 2005 he declared that 'any number of historians have incorporated the history of the [Tatar] Golden Horde into the history of Russia itself' and emphasized that Russians had sometimes fought alongside Tatars and vice versa, quoting Gumilev's eulogy of a 'great culture of the steppe' that united diverse peoples within a common civilization.[26] The same tone of homage appeared when Putin wished success on a congress in St Petersburg dedicated to 'the heritage of Lev Gumilev and the destiny of the peoples of Eurasia: history, the present and future perspectives': 'Possessing an exceptional aptitude for analysis, the talent of a genuine researcher and discoverer, Lev Gumilev made a unique contribution to the development of national and global scientific thinking.'[27]

Why this interest in Gumilev? Perhaps it is partly because Putin may have crossed paths with him in St Petersburg in the early 1990s, but it must also be because Gumilev was ferociously anti-Western. In a 1992 interview, he expressed the view that Russia's future was to be found in the building of a 'Eurasian power' and in the choice of good allies: 'The Turks and the Mongols can be sincere friends, but the English, the French and the Germans are only, I am convinced, Machiavellian exploiters.'[28] That same year, in St Petersburg Putin was starting his ascent to the heights of power.

Finally, it is worth noting that Gumilev, like Leontiev and Danilevsky, was set apart from other anti-Western thinkers and Eurasianists by his claim to scientific rigour, and it is by no means as sure as his supporters claim that he was 'the last of the Eurasianists', Soviet heir to the tsarist-era thinkers.[29] He developed what he termed a deterministic biology of peoples, a theory far removed from the thinking of his predecessors, who believed that different peoples could coalesce in a single region and that there was a potent interaction between geography and these peoples' lives. What interested Gumilev more was what he took to be the particular influence on a particular people of cosmic energy—arising from living creatures, minerals, solar activity and so on. Deeply naturalist in perspective, Gumilev believed in genetics, not in the influence of environment on humans. The idea of a cosmic force transmitted to a given people is at the heart of one of his fundamental notions, 'passionarity', and this is precisely what Putin celebrated in his 2012 annual address to the Federal Assembly.

Facing the Assembly at the end of the first year to witness significant opposition to Putin and his policies, the Russian president applied Gumilev's ideas to his analysis of global processes:

> Competition for resources is becoming more intense. And I can assure you and want to emphasize that this competition will not be limited only to metals, oil and gas, but above all will focus on human resources and intelligence. Who will take the lead and who will remain outsiders, and inevitably lose their independence, will depend not only on the economic potential, but primarily on the will of each nation, on its inner energy, which Lev Gumilev termed 'passionarity': the ability to move forward and to embrace change.[30]

Here, Putin has opted for the most scientistic version of the Eurasianist idea. Essentially, in his eyes, the passionarity of the Russian people is more vital than the egalitarian co-existence of diverse Eurasian communities, which was foremost in the minds of the doctrine's founders.

In this context, as Alexander Morozov underlines, we should note that since 2012 new terms have entered the president's lexicon—'that of "Russian civilization" or even a "civilizational code", which suggests that civilization is a living organism with its own genetic code.'[31] Putin has notably spoken of 'our historic code, our national character',[32] and the historian of philosophy Nikolai Plotnikov confirms a shift towards scientism. Putin's speech of 18 March 2014 celebrating the recent annexation of Crimea

> exposed the idea of Russian man exhibiting a superiority that is not only cultural but also genetic—more resilient, etc. This socio-biological analysis of a people is a legacy of Danilevsky and Gumilev. One can't liken this type of ideology to national socialism, since it's not an ideology of destroying others. That said, this theory does affirm not only social and moral but genetic Russian superiority over other peoples.[33]

7

FALSE FRIENDS

DOSTOEVSKY AND BERDYAEV

The time has now come to ponder a pair of particularly delicate cases. Two of the most important Russian authors of the nineteenth and twentieth centuries are regularly deployed by Putin and by representatives of the 'conservative turn': Fyodor Dostoevsky (1821–88) and the philosopher Nikolai Berdyaev (1874–1948). Their portraits appear side by side on a website for 'conservative political thought', Russian Idea—also the title of a work by Berdyaev. Dostoevsky, if we are to believe the president's declarations, stands beside Tolstoy, Chekov, Lermontov and Mandelstam in the pantheon of Putin's favourite writers;[1] he has claimed to *Paris Match* that he 'read[s] with pleasure the Russian classics, especially Dostoevsky and Tolstoy'.[2]

Putin has deployed such repeated references judiciously, but too mechanically and too circumstantially for them to appear profound. In 2006 in Dresden, the

German city where he worked for the KGB and whose museum Dostoevsky visited with great attention during his European wanderings, Putin inaugurated a monument to the great writer. Praising the author, whom he claimed was a [gentle] pro-European, he declared:

> One of Dostoevsky's mottos was as follows: 'beauty will save the world.' He aimed above all for harmony between people. And in that sense this [statue] is a symbolic gesture from the German authorities, the authorities of Dresden. It means that we live in a united European cultural space.[3]

If this was pathos worthy of a Dostoevskian dreamer, a few months later Putin used the writer to make a rather more vindictive point. Drawing on Dostoevsky's 'politico-philosophical definition of Russia's European destiny'[4] and his famous speech in honour of Pushkin some weeks after the latter's death, Putin argued that 'Europe would never be itself in the world without Russia and, at the same time ... Russia would never cease its "longing for Europe".'[5] This call for European integration not to leave Russia out in the cold shows how flexible Putin's use of Dostoevsky can be.

It was the conservative turn from 2012 that really offered Dostoevsky a new role, as the author Putin had admired for his Christ-like mildness and ecumenical vision of the bond uniting Russia and Europe suddenly became, or became once more, a fierce adversary of the liberal, socialist and pro-West intelligentsia. In other words, the author of *The Brothers Karamazov* had suddenly become the author of *Demons*, his satirical, anti-nihilist novel. On 25 May 2014, the very evening of the Ukrainian presidential election that would signal the victory of the pro-European movement, the TV channel Russia-1 broadcast the first episodes of a new series: a heavily publicized adaptation of *Demons*. Its director, Vladimir Khotinenko, who was on the Moscow Orthodox Patriarchate Council for Culture, was sending a very clear message to pro-European intellectuals: the country doesn't like you. The novel tells of a plot by unscrupulous revolutionaries against the legitimate authorities in a provincial town. These cynical and brutal young nihilists, encouraged by ridiculous Westernized intellectuals, end up assassinating an Orthodox nationalist militant.

Today's liberals, however, were not taken in. On the radio station Echo of Moscow, the writer, satirical poet and anti-Putin chronicler Dmitry Bykov pushed back against the adaptation, calling it 'a crime against the text and its context'. He found it stupid to 'label intellectuals who thirst for freedom as "demons"'.[6] Anti-Western voices, meanwhile, relished the attack on the despised 'liberals', and, according to the science fiction writer Sergei Lukyanenko, 'events in Ukraine correspond exactly to what Dostoevsky wrote. We're dealing with a classic situation of anti-Russian struggle ... But the Ukrainians are part of the Russian people.'[7] Now,

Dostoevsky was being openly appropriated for ideological purposes. Could one of Russia's most celebrated authors, who has left a lasting mark on national cultural and philosophical life—could Dostoevsky, who has inspired all great Russian thinkers from Solovyov to Berdyaev, possibly be a Putinist?

* * *

For supporters of the conservative turn, there is no question about it. Dostoevsky, who had been a socialist-inclined pro-European in his youth before living through the penal colony and banishment, attacked the Western ideologies of his time: revolutionary socialism, anarchism, utilitarianism, positivism and scientism, which he saw as variants of a destructive atheism. In *Demons*, he wanted to trace the lineage from the idealistic Westernizing liberals of the 1840s to the following generation, violent and hyper-negative. Most importantly, in the 1870s he moved closer to the most reactionary of circles. It was then that he produced his *Writer's Diary*, which contained his most sensational declarations, freely quoted by today's 'Russian way' partisans. He wrote an apologia of Nikolay Danilevsky, who had made the same ideological journey as he had, from Fourierism to reaction, and praised Danilevsky's *Russia and Europe*, 'an excellent work'.

However, he did complain of its 'lack of clarity and firmness' on the 'future status of Constantinople'.[8] For

Dostoevsky, Istanbul should have been taken from the Turks and placed under the exclusive control of Russia and not, as Danilevsky proposed, of all Slavic nations. The novelist had a messianic view of Russia's role, one in which the virtues of the Russian people, allied to the strength of the Empire, would save the world. The Russian soul and the roots of the nation were ceaselessly glorified. Dostoevsky ultimately seemed so obsessed by what he perceived as an alliance between the Roman Catholic Church and socialist forces that he immersed himself in religious theory that bordered on delirium. Even a supporter of the conservative turn like Boris Mezhuev considers that Dostoevsky, fanatical in his struggle against Catholicism, has no influence in this respect on current Russian policy, which is far from planning a holy war against Rome.

Yet this picture is largely incomplete. It cannot be denied that Dostoevsky was very close in the 1870s to the most reactionary of doctrines, nor that he developed a pro-Orthodox religious theory. But Dostoevsky the man, the *engagé* intellectual and novelist, amounted to much more than that. In terms of political and philosophical ideas, one need only remember that after his return from the penal colony in the early 1860s he founded a journal to offer an alternative theory to both the Slavophile and Westernizer movements. It should also be recalled that Dostoevsky underwent a change in the second half of the 1870s, when he became closely interested in, and sometimes sympathetic to, the new revolutionary generation, who were moving away from nihilism in favour of a populism that was sometimes almost mystical. Besides, Dostoevsky's nationalist thinking proved much more complex than Danilevsky's theory of 'cultural-historical types'. Danilevsky insisted on the irreducible specificity of types and on the distance between them, writing notably in *Russia and Europe*: 'It is difficult for a Frenchman or an Englishman to think in the German way, and it is even more difficult for a Slav on account of the ethnographic distance.'[9] The Dostoevskian view of Russian man was diametrically opposed to this. In *The Adolescent* (1875), a novel that dramatizes Dostoevsky's ideal of 'universal Russia' in the form of the *déraciné* aristocrat Versilov, we read:

> any Frenchman can serve not only his France, but even mankind, solely on condition that he remains most of all a Frenchman; the same applies to the Englishman and the German. Only the Russian ... is capable of becoming most Russian precisely only when he is most European. That is our most essential national distinction from all the rest, and in this respect Russia is like nowhere else. In France I'm a Frenchman, with a German I'm a German, with an ancient Greek a Greek, and by that very fact I'm most Russian.[10]

Of course, this capacity for structural openness only confirms Dostoevsky's belief in the superiority of the Russians over the Germans or French, but it also has the advantage of avoiding any pseudo-science of peoples; it contains no ethical dimension and is more dialectical than a theory of genetic Russian pre-eminence. Dostoevsky never forgot that he was a St Petersburger and a rootless intellectual, fond of Western culture. The idea of the Russian nation as the victory of fragility, he thought, would allow the old debate between Westernizers and Slavophiles to be transcended. The Russian universality that he wished for had in fact only been made possible by the 'broadening of outlook'[11] on Europe inaugurated by Peter the Great, an intellectual broadening unrivalled by any other people. The Slavophiles, with their withdrawal into the purely national, were incapable of thinking in terms of Russia's universal mission. The Westernizers, due to their interpretation of this broadening as an imitation of the West, did not understand that it was serving to accelerate the redeeming destiny of the Russian Orthodox idea. This was the open vision of nationalism that Dostoevsky defended in the 'Pushkin Speech' quoted by Putin: a call for the construction of a Russian prowess more cultural and peaceful than political or military.

The least one can say about Dostoevsky is that he was madder, more profound, and more of a genius than Danilevsky. He was a nationalist and a Pan-Slavist, intolerant of other confessions and faiths, but at the same time a universalist, a proponent of collective consciousness and profoundly European. This almost incomprehensible 'broadness'[12] obviously finds its most acute expression in his novels. Many readers of *A Writer's Diary* prefer its impromptu pieces of fiction such as 'Bobok', 'The Dream of a Ridiculous Man' and 'The Meek One', altogether more striking than its nationalist proclamations and heavy-going analyses. Dostoevsky the novelist shatters all attempts to make his message definitively ideological. *Demons* would not be a major work of world literature if it could accurately be reduced to an attack on liberals, for the human reality that Dostoevsky portrays goes beyond political labels. In one of the novel's most mysterious characters, the leader of the revolutionaries Pyotr Verkhovensky, one can see either a 'nihilist' or a 'socialist'. But above all we see a neat, precise and meticulous little being, at times ceremonious, at others inconsiderate; a man thirsty for power who has mastered better than anyone the minute physical signs of domination and humiliation. He uses his talent as an actor to play himself, and to pass for an ordinary fellow. He flatters, lies, manipulates, ridicules, controls, spies, gives orders and brutalizes. If Dostoevsky had created him today, he perhaps would have made him an ex-spy turned national leader.

Ultimately,Dostoevsky's novel is essentially polyphonic.[13] He gives an airing to the opinions furthest from those attributed to the author himself. The voices of enemies of the state, nihilists, child rapists, old gossips and universalist idiots are heard as much as the others.

Sometimes Dostoevsky gets caught up in the game, and this is when he is at his most impressive. In a letter written when he was working on *The Brothers Karamazov*, the novelist revealed that he had wanted to attack the 'blasphemy' of Ivan's poem *The Grand Inquisitor*, 'but I myself feel it, and understand that it wins out'.[14] Some say that he also suggested a planned sequel in which the novel's hero, the young Christian Alyosha, would become a regicide. Dostoevsky is too immense a novelist to be claimed for any single ideological discourse, let alone for pseudo-scientific nationalism.

* * *

Now we come to the second major Russian thinker who has been the victim of certain misapprehensions. On 12 December 2013, Putin cited Nikolai Berdyaev (1874–1948) in his annual address to the Federal Assembly, at the very moment that he was laying his cards on the table when it came to

> the values of traditional families, real human life, including religious life, not just material existence but also spirituality, the values of humanism and global diversity. Of course, this is a conservative position. But speaking in the words of Nikolai Berdyaev, the point of conservatism is not that it prevents movement forward and upward, but that it prevents movement backward and downward, into chaotic darkness and a return to a primitive state.[15]

This is a quotation from *The Philosophy of Inequality*, a work written in 1918 as a reaction to the October Revolution of the previous year. The fifth 'letter' of the book, 'On Conservatism', comprises a eulogy of that concept. Boris Mezhuev, one of the ideologues of the conservative turn, revealed mysteriously to me that 'somebody [in power] feels very close to this work'.[16]

Berdyaev represents the 'religious renaissance' of Russian philosophy that took place at the end of the nineteenth century. Following in the footsteps of Vladimir Solovyov, he created, with Father Sergei Bulgakov, Father Pavel Florensky, Semyon Frank, Lev Shestov and others, an original form of religious philosophy that was in no way nationalist or imperialist. Like several important figures of his generation, Berdyaev was initially revolutionary and close to Marxism, but later distanced himself from Marxism and mixed metaphysics with an existential approach. Emigrating to Germany and then France, he participated actively in the intellectual life of the interwar years and became famous in Europe. Never really forgotten in the USSR, he has been one of the most popular 'thinkers from before' since perestroika, and now has found himself an emblem of Putinism.

As we know (see Chapter 4), very soon after the 2013 presidential address, conferences on conservatism were organized for Kremlin staff and members of the ruling party, United Russia. According to a member of the presidential administration, the 'chapter "On Conservatism" was mandatory reading for officials, since this was the very text that Vladimir Putin had quoted. To understand what the president has in mind, it is indispensable to take note of his original source.'[17] This conservative university for the political elite reached its apogee in May 2014, when 'Berdyaev Days' were organized in the Moscow region for the first time. The coordinating institution, the Institute of Socio-Economic and Political Research, was close to the Kremlin. Its aim was as unambiguous as any presidential imperial decree: to demonstrate that conservatism had all the qualities required to set the direction of Russian politics, and that major names like Berdyaev supported it.

The problem is that Berdyaev had nothing to do with Ilyin, Leontiev, Danilevsky or Gumilev. Berdyaev, opposed to any scientistic reduction of human history, was not, in fact, a conservative. *The Philosophy of Inequality* was a text written under the shock of the Bolshevik revolution in October 1917, which Berdyaev condemned with as much force as he had supported its February predecessor. Several days after the second, successful revolution, he wrote a text entitled 'Has There Been a Revolution in Russia?', in which he deplored what he called an eruption of savagery, which had brought no regeneration: 'In the souls of people and in the soul of the people,' he wrote, 'in the wellsprings of creative energy nothing has changed, nothing new has been born. All the same old instincts are active, all the same old feelings. The new man is not being born. Nor has any new soul been born within the elements of the Revolution.'[18] Berdyaev was openly opposed to the new power structure, which he believed was inclined to install a dictatorship. Above all, he thought, this event showed the dangers of ideology in social and political life:

> The moral however, which the Russian 'Revolution' teaches, is quite simple and elementary, though also bitter for us. It has become necessary to part company with many of the Russian illusions, with the Slavophiles, the Populists, the Tolstoyans, the lofty-minded anarchists, the revolutionary-messianists, etc, etc. It is necessary to repent and be humbled, to sacrificially admit the elementary truth of Westernism, the truth of culture, the harsh truth of law and norms. ... When the Russian people awaken from their hypnosis and spiritually sober up, they will comprehend that every great struggle in the world is a spiritual struggle, a clash of varying ideas.[19]

While clearly hostile to bolshevism, the philosopher had also been critical for several years of the Russian atheist intelligentsia, which had scorned important philosophical questions in favour of revolutionary activism. In his contribution to *Vekhi* (*Landmarks*), a collection of articles published in 1909, Berdyaev lamented the malady of this intellectual elite: 'Love for a levelling egalitarian justice, for social good, for the people's happiness, paralyzed love of truth and nearly annihilated interest in truth.'[20] Berdyaev had nothing against social ideals, but wished that they did not prevent a profound philosophical interrogation of the 'meaning of the creative act', of 'the destiny of man' (both titles of his works)—of the ontological liberty that he situated at the heart of human existence. He wanted not to suppress the social question, but to rebuild the social upon a metaphysical foundation.

The Philosophy of Inequality defends conservatism against revolutionary chaos, but in a purely philosophical sense. Berdyaev is specific at the start of the 'Fifth Letter': 'I want to speak now about conservatism, neither as a political direction nor as a political party, but as an eternal, religious and ontological principle in all human society.' He emphasizes that 'the nature of conservatism is misunderstood, not only by its enemies, but also by some of its supporters',[21] who see in it a political programme of power, rather than simply fidelity to the past. For Berdyaev, it is a matter of eulogizing the idea of rootedness in history and love of culture against violent but artificial convulsions over the ages, rather than the utopia of the *tabula rasa* and the new man. Here there is no nationalism, no theory of the superiority of Russian man, no proclamation of 'traditional values' against supposed deviants—just an appeal, in the totalitarian context of the revolution, not to shatter a cultural inheritance. Many 'liberals' today would easily find their views reflected in this agenda.

What's more, Berdyaev's philosophy revolves around a central idea: irreducible freedom. This is a notion more profound and ontologically rich than that of free will. As he put it in *Dostoevsky*, 'the truth about freedom is inexpressible';[22] it is a life principle, a sort of grace, and not a rational discourse. He rejects on principle any attempt to impose constraint on the opinions and actions of men, the preserve, he believes, of Dostoevsky's Grand Inquisitor—he rejects, in other words, ideology, or voluntary servitude. It was for this reason that Berdyaev often opposed the official Church, the bearer of a conformist spirit contradictory to the believer's essential freedom.

It is no coincidence, then, that enemies of the alliance prevalent today between Russian Church and state also refer to Berdyaev. Take, for instance, certain members of the Pussy Riot collective, who famously performed a 'punk prayer' in Moscow's Christ the Saviour Cathedral on 21 February 2012. The balaclava-clad young women chanted, 'Mary Mother of God is with us in protest!' before being arrested. While serving her sentence in a penal colony in Mordovia, after an August 2012 conviction of 'hooliganism motivated by religious hatred', Nadezhda Tolokonnikova, one of the group's leaders, corresponded with the neo-communist philosopher Slavoj Žižek.[23] In her letter of 23 February 2013, she wrote in length about a philosopher who is hardly one of Žižek's everyday points of reference:

> Nikolai Berdyaev wrote in *Self-Knowledge*: 'Truths, as articles imposed on me, as realities falling onto me from above, do not exist. Truth is also a path, a life. Truth is spiritual conquest. Truth is known in freedom and through freedom.' He also wrote, 'I understand Christianity to be a rebellion against the world and its laws.' And he wrote, 'Sometimes, a nightmarish thought would occur to me: what if the orthodoxy of slavery is correct? That would mean I was already dead. So I'd quickly dispense with the notion.'

'On this point,' she continued, 'there is no difference between the statements of Pussy Riot and those of this great political philosopher. In 1898, Berdyaev was arrested on charges of agitating for the Social Democrats, indicted for "designs on the overthrow of the government and the Church", and exiled from Kiev for three years to Vologda. When the World Spirit touches you, don't think you can walk away unscathed.' Perhaps Pussy Riot, with their prayer against the 'servile orthodoxy' of the prelates, wanted to be faithful to another of Berdyaev's injunctions in *The Philosophy of Inequality*, which calls for 'energy' in 'religious creation.'[24] In any case, it is clear that in today's Russia, the philosopher has become a major reference point for those who challenge Vladimir Putin's politics. Had he known, he might not have launched such a rash takeover bid of Berdyaev's thought.

8

PUTIN'S EMPIRE

In 2007, President Putin denied that Russia had any imperial vocation or mission. He addressed the 'idea of Pan-Slavism' and the ideological foundations of both tsarist Russia (in order, 'the monarchy, the link with the people and Orthodoxy') and the Soviet empire, and claimed that 'Today's Russia has no intention of following the tsarist example, and even less intention of following the Soviet example.'[1] He made himself very clear: 'I therefore have no wish to see our people, much less our leadership, seized by missionary ideas.' A year later, his successor Dmitry Medvedev invaded Georgia, placing under Russian protection two secessionist territories, South Ossetia and Abkhazia, whose independence from Georgia was recognized only by Moscow, Venezuela, Nicaragua and the Micronesian republic of Nauru (in return for Russian aid worth US$50 million).[2]

Since the 2014 annexation of Crimea and the war in eastern Ukraine, in which Russian troops took part, tensions have grown between Russia and its neighbours, increasingly fearful of acts of destabilization or even military aggression. Ukraine's President Poroshenko (2014–) claims that Putin told him in September 2014 that 'if [he] wanted, Russian troops could arrive within two days, not only in Kiev, but also in Riga, Vilnius, Tallinn, Warsaw and Bucharest';[3] in other words, in EU and NATO member states. Several days earlier, the then US president Barack Obama had sought to reassure the Eastern European NATO states, warning unambiguously that 'the defence of Tallinn and Riga and Vilnius is just as important as the defence of Berlin and Paris and London', adding, 'You lost your independence once before. With NATO, you will never lose it again.'[4]

The game Putin was playing certainly contained a good deal of bluff and swagger, but the fact remained that the international climate had utterly changed, and there was only one reason for it. During the Maidan popular revolt in Kiev in the autumn and winter of 2013–14, many Ukrainians had warned of the Russian imperialist peril. Few, if anyone, took them seriously in the West. Who could have guessed that the Russian reaction to the victory of pro-European forces would be the deliberate seizure of Crimea, and the fomenting of civil war in Donbass and other eastern and southern regions of Ukraine? If the worst had happened now—a conflict in Europe itself, provoking tensions between Russia and the West that we had thought were buried forevermore at the end of the Cold War—then logic said that it could happen again, and even spread. The invasion of territories by the Russian military, whether in covert, hybrid or open war, is no longer unthinkable.

The philosophical origins of Putinism, however diverse they may be, all rest on two pillars: the idea of empire and the justification of war. This is the ideological core common to the Soviet system, the 'White' imperialism of Ilyin, the conservatism of Leontiev (in several of his works), the Pan-Slavism of Danilevsky, and Eurasianism, both the founders' version and Dugin's today. For evidence of this we need look no further than one far-right ideologue, who has been very influential for the last quarter-century. Born in 1938, Alexander Prokhanov founded the far-right daily newspaper *Den* (The Day) and, after it was banned, *Zavtra* (Tomorrow). Though Prokhanov is too extremist to be part of Putin's inner circle, he is still a widely followed commentator. He is not 'Putin's teacher', as he assured me during an interview, but he does think that his ideas 'are starting to have an effect', especially among the president's advisers.

Indeed, recent events have seemed to give weight to Prokhanov's analysis and prophecies, which swells his audience further. In a theory that eschews both textual detail and the nuances of philosophical doctrine, he offers a highly vulgarized version of the Slavophile tradition, which can be summed up in three words: messianism, imperialism and belligerence. The 'Russian way,' he says, germinated from the fifteenth century 'with the theory that "Moscow, the third Rome", was destined to replace Constantinople, after its fall [in 1453], at the head of Christianity. It crystallized in the nineteenth century. It then metamorphosed again after the collapse of the Russian Empire.' Four empires followed one another: the Russia of Kiev and Novgorod, then Muscovy, then the Romanovs and finally the Soviet empire. 'Today,' Prokhanov claims, a fifth empire is emerging,' and it is founded on three axioms.

According to the first, 'Russia is by nature an empire with living, breathing frontiers', which vindicates any annexations. 'Putin may not yet have used the term "empire", but he is beginning to fulfil it as a reality. It started with the war against Georgia in 2008. Events in Crimea and Ukraine have been the continuation of this trend.' The second axiom is that 'Russia has always obeyed the idea of divine justice'. 'There is a Russian messianism,' Prokhanov asserts, 'and there is thus not only a strategic but at the same time a spiritual conflict between East and West.' Finally, the third axiom is that 'the conservative values promoted by Putin on the individual, the family and relations with nature clash head-on with Western modernism. Russia is theocentric where the West is anthropocentric.'

In short, 'Putin is restoring to its original imperial form the Russian state that disappeared after the collapse of the USSR.' What happened in Ukraine was perfectly logical and Moscow's response was legitimate: 'Russia is coming to the aid of Ukraine's [ethnic] Russians and Russian-speakers just as the West came to the aid of the Maidan revolutionaries, with money and a whole arsenal of other means. We are only imitating the West.' And tomorrow? 'The confrontation with the West is going to continue and get worse. Russia will turn increasingly towards China and India to build an anti-Western front. Two enemy camps are forming and we are moving towards a new world war. Only God will decide the outcome,' he concluded.[5]

* * *

It remains to be seen precisely what form this new empire might take. Here again, philosophical and ideological sources help to identify possible scenarios. The first model that springs to mind is that of the Soviet Union, which Vladimir Putin knew, loved and served for forty years of his life. Like a large section of his fellow citizens, he certainly regrets the passing of a time when one could travel without difficulty between Moscow, Tallinn, Lviv, Tbilisi or Tashkent, in the same trains and planes, without crossing borders or changing currency, using the same language of communication and driving the same cars—a country where everyone watched the same films, had the same rituals, shared common references and sometimes even a common ideal. Despite ideological oppression,[6] doublespeak, censorship, difficulties in travelling outside the USSR, absence of freedom, repression, prison camps and psychiatric hospitals for dissidents, Soviet life has been idealized by part of the population.[7] As no memory work has been done on the Soviet past, and as imprisoned dissidents were hastily freed in 1985 and then practically disappeared from the political scene, the socio-economic difficulties of the 1990s and Putin's unofficial restoration of the USSR have generated nostalgia. Apart from the comforts of a cocooned life, there is also a yearning for the power of the Soviet Union, widely overestimated but celebrated ad nauseam. The loss of Eastern Europe, the pitiable return of Russian troops to rundown barracks, the collapse of state services, and the overall atmosphere of permanent crisis and disorder have humiliated those brought up with a collective self-image bordering on megalomania.

The creation of the Eurasian Union certainly gives the impression of a return to the Soviet empire, particularly if the rouble becomes it common currency. But even in the most optimistic scenarios, it seems very unlikely that the Baltic States, Georgia and certain countries of Central Asia, without even mentioning the most important piece of the puzzle, Ukraine, would willingly participate in such a resurrection. Moscow's Kievskaya metro station, its major Riga Station and its famous restaurant Uzbekistan will long remain signifiers that have lost their meaning. The cement that held together this lost multi-ethnic and interdenominational empire was a modernist and unifying ideology: Marxist-Leninist communism. From Riga to Ashgabat, from Erevan to Kishinev, work was underway to create a classless society, freed of religious alienation and united in its devotion to a common history of the revolution and its heroes. Without such a unifying ideology, the renaissance of a 'red' empire is unfeasible, and it is implausible that Eurasianism, a plural, complex and less mobilizing doctrine, might come to replace it.

Even if the communist idea attracts many young people in the former Soviet empire, the return to power of the communists in a traditional form is hardly imminent. The powerful vector of modernizing and socialist emancipation has given way to the championing of identities. We have tumbled into a new global paradigm. In Russia, only those elements compatible with today's new identitarian ideology will be conserved: Stalin, considered as a patriotic figure who is preferred to the internationalist Lenin; the victory in the Second World War; the exaltation of national greatness; general patriotism, valuing of heroism and the spirit of sacrifice; cultural intellectualism; and social conservatism. This excludes Stalin's dialectical and historical materialism, the 'official' Soviet interpretation of Marxism.

If not Soviet nostalgia, then what might be the guiding principles of a new Russian empire? Nikolay Danilevsky advocated Pan-Slavism; however, though the memory of pan-Slavic fervour during the Yugoslav wars has not entirely faded—notably for Putin himself, who can never forgive the West for the 1999 conflict in Kosovo—it is still hard to envisage the Czechs or the Poles participating of their own free will in a Slavic empire led by Russia. One traditional link in the chain of Russian Pan-Slavism, and one that Putin is seemingly reviving today, is Bulgaria. A member of NATO since 2004 and of the European Union since 2007, this country, long 'protected' by its Russian 'big brother', has endured strong pressures since the Ukrainian crisis. Dependent on Russia for energy, Bulgaria has been caught in the crossfire. Its plan to rid itself of its Soviet-era military planes recently provoked brusque exchanges between the two countries. If a Pan-Slavic rebirth were to take place, it might begin with the destabilization of Bulgaria, where the population has always been divided between pro-Europeans and pro-Russians.

Pan-Slavism is not a very realistic option either, then—so why not place the new empire under the banner of Orthodoxy? This would theoretically allow Russia to discard Catholic Poland and other non-majority-Orthodox countries (the Czech Republic, the Baltic States, Slovakia), and concentrate on culturally closer peoples such as Serbs, Bulgarians, Belarusians and Ukrainians, as well as to seduce the Georgians. This could even arouse the sympathies of the Greeks and Romanians. For Putin, 'many different ethnic groups ...

are united by the Orthodox faith' and 'the Church's importance goes beyond the borders of today's Russian Federation'. Particularly, it unites Russia with 'the peoples of Ukraine and Belarus', as all three share 'common historical moral and spiritual roots'.[8]

The great advantage of an Orthodox empire would be access to a powerful ideology. Since his arrival in power in 2000, Putin, in coordination with the Moscow Patriarchate, has broadly instrumentalized Orthodox Christianity, which was historically hostile to nationalism, turning it into his ideological armed wing. Exhibitions of relics draw huge crowds, religious conformism is dominant, and self-confessed free thinkers are sometimes poorly thought of in Russia today. Any artistic expression that could be perceived as transgressive in terms of religion is severely censured. The Russian Orthodox Church attached to the Moscow Patriarchate is nowadays actively legitimist and conservative, with a very conspicuous media presence as it disseminates its often reactionary messages.

I spoke to Father Vsevolod Chaplin, who long presided over the Church's department for relations with society. Prone to sensationalist statements, he has called for the creation of 'Orthodox militias'[9] and has criticized the 'Russophobia'[10] of intellectuals. He has called on 'Russian woman' to dress modestly, explaining that

> if she wears a miniskirt, she may provoke not only a Caucasian but even a Russian. If she is drunk, she will

> provoke him all the more. And if on top of all that she actively goes out looking to interact with people, and if she is later surprised that the interaction ends in rape, then she's even more in the wrong.[11]

Chaplin also purports to be very active against the 'paedophile lobby' and has proposed banning Nabokov's *Lolita*.[12] He is militantly in favour of a 'Christian model' that can serve as an alternative to the secularized and liberal West, where the media elites of 'pseudo-democracies' have imposed their own favouring of an ultraliberal economy and abandonment of family values.

Chaplin told me that 'after the 1990s, when everything concerned with the past, especially Soviet collectivization, was rejected, there was a return to Orthodox ideals such as a spiritual community (*sobornost*, the central concept of Slavophile thought), collective property, repudiation of materialism and law in the religious sense.' Unfortunately, he lamented, this revival has not yet transferred to politics, even though the Moscow Patriarchate is working on it. According to Chaplin, 'Russia can build its own economic way, different from what the West has been constructing for two centuries: an economy freed from the diktat of finance and moneylending, one based on self-sufficiency and in accordance with Christian ideals.' Essentially, the idea is to rehabilitate communist principles, but in order to champion, in all domains, a 'Christian civilization' that goes beyond a mere national entity—it could 'take shape everywhere'.[13]

For all that, is an Orthodox or Christian empire really a possibility? It certainly wouldn't be easy. Firstly, Russia is a multi-confessional entity. In dreaming of an empire founded on religious principles, Putin would alienate all the country's Muslim populations—not to mention its Buddhists and followers of Shamanism. He has played the religion card to guarantee the support of the Orthodox majority and, when necessary, to gratify the Greek or Serb people. Many Armenians, meanwhile, recognize Russia's traditional role as their protector from Muslim or Turkish-speaking countries. In a word, Orthodoxy is just one card in the diverse Russian deck.

Perhaps Putin could assemble an empire of all the ethnic Russians dispersed across the former Soviet republics? He has always argued that the 'geopolitical catastrophe' of the collapse of the USSR lay in the humanitarian issue of many Russian populations left outside their homeland, in sometimes hostile republics. In his declarations he has often repeated that 'We are not indifferent to the status of our compatriots', whether in Ukraine, Central Asia or even in 'the Baltic States, which still have the entirely uncivilised concept of a "non-citizen" ... deprived of political and human rights and freedoms'.[14] It was to defend the 'Russians of Ukraine' from attacks by the 'fascist junta in Kiev' that Russian forces took covert part in the ongoing war in eastern and southern Ukraine.

Another possible vehicle for empire-building lies with the Russophones (who are not all ethnically Russian).

We will see in due course that they justify a Russian policy of influence in many countries, and could also become a factor in a Russian project of imperial unity. As early as 2002, Putin was already claiming that 'a crushing majority of citizens of the countries of the CIS [Commonwealth of Independent States, the grouping of ten former Soviet republics created at the fall of the USSR] consider the Russian language practically as their second mother tongue. In other words, there's no language barrier between us.'[15] Yes, twenty years after the fall of the USSR, Russian language usage was in retreat, especially among the youngest, but for Putin it remained a 'bridge'[16] between different, 'historically linked'[17] states such as Russia and Turkmenistan. But here again, an ethnic or linguistic criterion is not enough to define a unique, coherent imperial principle. Putin's former economic adviser Andrei Illarionov stresses that 'South Ossetia and Abkhazia, for example, are not Russian lands. The same goes for Georgia and Armenia, which Russia is trying to get hold of by handing out Russian Federation passports to anyone who asks, thus multiplying the number of Russian citizens there.' Furthermore, the first steps towards a new empire, taken with the Russo-Georgian conflict of 2008, had nothing to do with the Russian language, or Orthodoxy. According to Illarionov, 'national or religious factors are of secondary importance in this imperial policy.[18]

* * *

The most ideologically consistent project seems to be that of the Eurasian Union, which is under construction and possesses a solid philosophical foundation. The idea of a Eurasian empire offers several advantages: particularly, welcoming different peoples, languages and religions and thus essentially eschewing nationalism; and giving substance to the 'Asian turn' of Russian politics, in other words rejecting the West and seeking alliance with China. The final asset is that the notion of Eurasia is sufficiently debated, and hence vague, to allow any necessary adjustments, such as one day including Bulgaria or 'going down again' towards Afghanistan. Putin has evoked 'the immense territory of Eurasia from the Baltic and Carpathians to the Pacific Ocean',[19] and Eurasia remains a plastic concept that allows interplay between the geography of an objective space and different, competing theories. Politically, Eurasia is an ad hoc construction.

Putin has given thought to the Eurasian Economic Union and to a 'civilizational Eurasian union' since first winning the presidency. He sees no contradiction between this eastward shift and the affirmation of traditional 'Christian values' and even believes that Russia brings the two civilizations together. 'Russia is a unique country,' he has explained,

> in that part of its territory is in Asia and a large part is in Europe. Christian values form the foundation of Russian culture and in this sense Russia is a European country. But Russia is also home to 15 million Muslims,

> a large part of our territory is in Asia, and we also have interests in Asia.[20]

Putin sees his country as the pivot of Eurasia—to the West, champion of a Christian Europe that has seemingly lost its roots; to the East, Asia's centre of gravity. Russia, then, must act as leader of Eurasia for reasons beyond its geographical position: as a vast multi-ethnic country, Russia in itself represents a microcosm of it. Putin has declared that 'Russia, as a Eurasian country, is a unique example where the dialogue of cultural civilizations has developed in practice, and become a centuries-old tradition of state and public life.'[21] As a living symbol of the harmony of differences, Russia deserves to be the matrix of this future superpower. For Putin, this metaphysical model of diversity within unity, lengthily explored in late nineteenth-century Russian philosophy, stands in clear contrast to Anglo-Saxon (British and American) cultural, linguistic and political homogeneity. In time, then, Eurasia must replace the United States as the world's leading power.

Yet Putin has sometimes overlooked a key element: China, which Washington now considers its true political rival. The Russian president has also courted Beijing, claiming in July 2000 that 'China is a strategic partner for us in every sense of the term'.[22] This early, while Putin was still in his officially pro-European phase, he tended to nuance his words when addressing the Chinese: one month later, he hedged, 'Russia is a

European and Asian state. We pay respect to European pragmatism and eastern wisdom. That is why Russia's foreign policy will be balanced.' He added: 'Russia will always take support from its two pillars, the European and the Asian.'[23] But since 2012, as Putin has distanced himself from Europe, the turn towards China has been much more noticeable.

The Chinese president Xi Jinping (2013–),meanwhile, has been attentive to his Russian opposite number, selecting Russia for his first foreign visit in March 2013. Emphasizing the 'particular importance' of Russo-Chinese relations and the 'friendly atmosphere' of this 'historic visit', both protagonists of the meeting were sending a signal to the international community: China is more than Russia's primary trading partner. These two permanent members of the UN Security Council share a vision of the world: a reaffirmation of the principle of national sovereignty (whether in Syria, Tibet, Chechnya or elsewhere); defiance of Europe, seen to be in crisis; a desire to counter American domination; and a critical attitude to democratic values. Since the imposition of Western sanctions in 2014, Russia has wanted to further strengthen economic relations with China and has been dreaming of an alternative to the West in which the Eurasian doctrine could serve as an ideological basis. Yet it is highly doubtful that China would agree to bind itself to a Eurasian Union led by Russia, or even that it would be willing to cooperate in leading such a venture.

Rather, Putin's Eastern dream risks clashing with the increasingly unrestrained expressions of Chinese power.

Putin practises a fundamentally à la carte brand of imperialism. According to circumstance, he will conjure up nostalgia for the USSR, shared religious principles, the Russian language, a more vague 'Russianness', or the Eurasian project. The only common denominator in the president's various imperialist whims lies in the market economy. According to the economist Andrei Illarionov, 'Putin wants nothing to do with a red empire, nor a monarchical and patriarchal empire, nor a Eurasian empire. His vision is to build an efficient, modern and contemporary imperial system, founded on the free market'; close to that of the reformist politician and herald of a liberal empire Yegor Gaidar (1956–2009). Alexander Morozov is close to sharing Illarionov's point of view, suggesting that Putin aspires to

> set up a powerful economic union that will take the form of a confederation of states, with the goal of competing with the world's great economic powers. Putin's basic philosophy remains economy-centric. He wants to capture resources in order to participate in global capitalism with new forces. But he doesn't offer an alternative doctrine to global financial capitalism. He doesn't want to destroy it or to advocate something else.[24]

Whether the Moscow Patriarchate likes it or not, the empire that Putin is seeking rapidly to establish would be founded not on Orthodoxy but on the extension of the rouble—and such a structure would, of course, be dominated by Moscow.

According to the historian of philosophy Nikolai Plotnikov, there has also been no real turn towards Asia. 'The Eurasian Union is a replica of the European Union, nothing more. The prevailing feeling is that Russia is a European country, but that it is always possible to shut the window looking onto Europe and to move towards Asia for a while.' Putin's model, he believes, would be more like the British Empire in the late nineteenth and early twentieth centuries, which, after all, was the model endorsed by Ilyin and another Russian philosopher of that period, Pyotr Struve: 'A strong power must take care of economic growth in an expanding empire. On the one hand, in this model, power must be guided by law. But on the other, it self-identifies as expansionist.'[25] In other words, though it really does target the conquest of new lands, Putin's imperialism is not outdated, nostalgic or utopian; it blends, discreetly but absolutely, into the market economy.

* * *

What will be the next steps in this imperialist project, which began in 2008 and was confirmed in 2014? The annexation of Crimea and the war in Ukraine were the logical outcome of the failure of an imperialism based on persuasion. Putin's favourite Russian philosophers all thought of Ukraine as a major concern. Among the Slavophiles, Kiev was the inalienable source of Orthodoxy; Danilevsky viewed Ukrainians as the first of the 'Slavic brothers', and Ilyin declared that 'the Europeans ... dream of pushing Russia back towards Asia and of taking over its neighbouring European lands, notably Ukraine.' He predicted that 'Ukraine will have to choose between Poland and Russia.'[26] The Eurasianists, meanwhile, thought it absurd to want to detach Ukraine from Russia.[27] All these arguments reappear in Putin's own discourse on Ukraine, a litany of sometimes rather stifling declarations of love. This densely populated, vast and industrialized neighbour, with its prosperous agriculture, has been a subject of constant anxiety for Russia's leadership since its independence in 1991 and especially since the Orange Revolution of 2004. After the country's return to the Russian fold in 2010, with Viktor Yanukovych's election as president, Ukraine soon resumed its gravitation toward the West, with its decision to form a partnership with the European Union.

Putin's remarks on Russian-Ukrainian relations have been duly coaxing, but insistent: 'Our roots are to be found in Kievan Rus. Our shared fraternity is not a legend, but a historical fact,'[28] he stated in 2001. His vocabulary on the matter has wavered very significantly between opposing notions of proximity and union. He has spoken of the 'simple and natural desire to be side by side, to be together, to feel as if we are shoulder to shoulder.'[29] In Putin's mind, therefore, the Ukrainian-Russian border has become blurred, as if he could not accept the reality of the post-Soviet separation and of the Ukrainians' capacity to split from Moscow. In 2003 he addressed those 'whose activity wipes away all frontiers because cultural space has no borders. Especially between countries like Russia and Ukraine.'[30] Essentially ruling out a straightforward political relationship between two sovereign states, he made himself clear that same year:

> The relations between Russia and Ukraine are unique. We have a shared history. Most Ukrainian citizens link their destinies with Russia and many Russian citizens link their personal fates with Ukraine, where they have close relatives. This is a fact. Therefore we should build our relations by non-standard means and in non-standard ways.[31]

For this reason, when the Ukrainian majority decided to tie its future to the European Union, Russia's response in 2013–14 was also non-standard: the deployment to Donbass and the southern coast of 'little green men'—soldiers in unmarked uniforms, or clandestine troops.

The Orange Revolution of 2004, which was a victory for pro-European forces, was interpreted by Putin as 'an attempt to isolate the Russian Federation', which had 'no intention of annexing anybody'.[32] After his return to the presidency in 2012, he spared no effort in trying to persuade Ukraine to join the Eurasian Union, attempting to convince Viktor Yanukovych of the importance of such a decision for the Ukrainian economy:

> It is always a state's choice whether to associate with a given organization. But one must keep in mind the deepened level of cooperation [it would bring], of

> which we are both well aware and which you have just itemized: cooperation in atomic energy, energy in general, aeronautical construction, space, naval construction and perhaps other key industries.[33]

This was without even counting access to a huge market. But, by the end of 2012, Putin had no choice but to admit that Ukraine was dragging its feet: 'We were expecting to receive an official document from Ukraine in readiness for its membership of the customs union. We have not received it.'[34]

In March 2013, Putin was still coming up against Yanukovych's indecision and had to continue to make his case: 'From a socio-economic point of view, it seems to me today that there is not a single serious expert, in Ukraine or Russia, who doesn't think that it would be an unconditionally positive process for Ukraine.'[35] In the summer of 2013, Moscow's Orthodox patriarch journeyed to Kiev to celebrate the 1025th anniversary of Prince Vladimir's mass 'Baptism of Rus' (987 CE). Just before this visit, Putin made a clear reference to shared history and religion: 'The acceptance of Christianity [in Kiev] determined Russia's fate and choice of civilization.'[36] Two days later, in Kiev himself, he would evoke 'our spiritual unity'.[37] Russia's ties to Ukraine should be seen as indestructible, and Ukraine's departure towards Europe would cut Russia off from a part of itself.

As a last resort, seeing that neither pragmatic arguments nor historical allusions were being heeded, Putin shifted bluntly into the vocabulary of unity:

> Ukraine, without a doubt, is an independent state. That is how history has unfolded. But let's not forget that today's Russian statehood has roots in the Dnieper; as we say, we were baptized in the same Dnieper font. Kievan Rus started out as the foundation of the enormous future Russian state. We have common traditions, a common mentality, a common history and a common culture. We have very similar languages. In that respect, I want to repeat again, we are one people.[38]

The message was clear: any attempt to move away would be interpreted by Putin as a crime against Russian identity itself, and as a personal rift. And this time, it was heard—two months later, on 21 November 2013, President Yanukovych suspended negotiations over an association agreement with the European Union, which was due to be signed a week later. This unexpected decision launched the Maidan movement, which ended with violence against demonstrators and Yanukovych's flight to Russia in February 2014. Putin could do nothing about this development, but his reaction to it, in Crimea and then in eastern and central Ukraine, marked definitively the imperialist ideology that he had been developing over the years.

He gave a name to his action in Ukraine: the Novorossiya project. In April 2014, once the Crimea issue had been resolved in the name of 'the legitimate rights and interests of ethnic Russians and Russian speakers in the south-east of Ukraine', he pointed out that 'what was called Novorossiya (New Russia) in the tsarist days—Kharkov, Lugansk, Donetsk, Kherson, Nikolayev and Odessa—was not part of Ukraine back then. These territories were given to Ukraine in the 1920s by the Soviet government. Why? Who knows?' Perhaps, he suggested, it was time to take them back.[39]

This revived term, 'Novorossiya', was first coined during the Russian Empire's colonization of southern Ukraine. From more or less the mid-eighteenth century to 1830, several towns were founded, such as Ekaterinoslav (today Dnipro), Kherson, Mariupol and Odessa. Beyond the fighting in Donbass, Putin's Novorossiya plan sought to link Russia to Transnistria in Moldova, a region that has been occupied by pro-Russian forces since the end of the USSR. This would in turn open up the Crimean Peninsula. Linking Transnistria and Russia would entail occupying the whole of southern Ukraine, taking Mariupol on one side of the Peninsula and Odessa on the other. The minds behind Putin's Novorossiya—nationalist ideologues, Orthodox intellectuals and historians—have more or less retained the original meaning of the term.

In their eyes, the novelty of a Russian region in southern and western Ukraine would lie in the creation of a truly democratic country, freed of the corruption that afflicts 'old Russia', but benefiting from the resources of its big brother. Their fantasy is of a Russia regenerating itself from its new western territories. The Odessa-born historian Kirill Lipatov, who knows the Novorossiya theorists very well, is very sceptical, arguing: 'in other regions of this kind, protected by Russian troops but without official status or institutional stability—such as neighbouring Transnistria or South Ossetia and Abkhazia—criminal elements have immediately taken power.' His conclusion is a disenchanted one:

> If the Novorossiya project becomes reality, we will soon have a new criminal zone of arms trafficking, drugs etc. It will be a cancer on the body of Europe: a country without law, poor, isolated, hardly helped by Russia. What can we do about it? Nobody knows. And yet we're moving towards that situation full steam ahead.[40]

* * *

Given that Putin's politics are, as a matter of principle, unpredictable, what might be the next targets for his market-based imperialism? According to Alexander Morozov, the use of armed force should be the exception to the rule, since there are so many other means of exerting pressure on Russia's neighbours. 'A silent Anschluss could be carried out,' he explains, 'with referendums and voluntary unions, as happened in Crimea.' He believes that this

> could occur in the pro-Russian territories of Moldova such as Transnistria or Gagauzia, which are close to the Ukrainian border, or in Belarus, northern Kazakhstan, Kyrgyzstan or Armenia. There is nothing to suggest that Putin will be able to achieve all his goals, but we

> can at least be sure that he has had enough of drawn-out negotiations with his neighbours in the Commonwealth of Independent States. He has decided to take a more direct and more brutal path. In particular he will urge other governments, in the context of the global financial crisis, to abandon their currencies and adopt the rouble. That is the plan. Putin wants to move to a quicker building of the Eurasian Union.[41]

They may be members of NATO and may have received the public reassurance of then President Obama, but it should not be forgotten that the Baltic States are also a target of choice for Moscow. The Russian-speaking minorities in Latvia and Estonia (25 per cent of the population in 2014) could offer a pretext for destabilization. In the Caucasus, meanwhile, despite the departure of the pro-US Georgian president Mikheil Saakashvili in late 2013, the temptation persists to carve out a corridor to friendly Armenia through Georgian territory. The powder keg of Caucasian politics risks being reignited, and even Putin's allies within the Eurasian Union are worried. The perennial president of Kazakhstan, Nursultan Nazarbayev, may not have appreciated Putin's strange allusions when he congratulated his counterpart for having 'founded a state in a territory where there had never been a state'.[42] If Kazakhstan is such a young state, one might ask, what could happen on the death of its founder? In his 'How Shall We Reorganize Russia?', Solzhenitsyn suggested that the Russian-speaking territories in the north of the country should be joined to the Russian Federation as 'southern Siberia'. As for the countries that were forcibly recruited into the former Soviet bloc, such as Poland, they are fearful.

Putin, meanwhile, is exploring a new frontier further north, in a region that has become strategic: the Arctic. In discussion with students from the Lomonosov Northern (Arctic) Federal University in the Arkhangelsk region, he confirmed that 'there is growing interest in the region, particularly the Arctic region, and that interest will continue to increase',[43] since the Arctic offered 'great prospects' in terms of its commodities and the new navigation routes brought about by melting ice—not to mention the defence of Russia against American nuclear submarines. An island discovered by Russian pilots, lying in the Laptev Sea and baptized Yaya, was symbolically 'incorporated into the territory of Russia' in October 2014. Though minuscule, it 'allowed a significant extension of the limits of Russia's exclusive economic zone into the Arctic', according to state radio Voice of Russia.[44] Plans were announced in October 2014 for two brigades of 3,000 mechanized infantry to be stationed in the Yamal-Nenets region in the Arctic Circle, with military installations created in other Arctic territories.[45] The fight for the Great White North has just begun. It promises to be merciless.

* * *

Since 2014, war has, in any case, spread beyond Ukraine. On 9 May 2015, just as the patriotic exaltation of the annexation of Crimea was running out of steam, the Kremlin organized a grandiose ceremony to commemorate the seventieth anniversary of the USSR's victory over Nazi Germany in the 'Great Patriotic War'. New weaponry was on show in Red Square for the occasion. Several months later and following secret preparations, Putin moved into a new warzone: Syria. His professed wish was to put right what he presented at the United Nations, on 28 September 2015, as a succession of Western errors since the end of the Cold War: the Colour Revolutions and Arab Spring, both supposedly organized by the Americans, and the emergence of Islamic State, which Putin also argued had been encouraged and armed by Washington. As he unleashed his troops to defend the Syrian dictator Bashar al-Assad, this was the first time that Russia had projected its power beyond the ex-USSR since the war in Afghanistan (1979–89). While the Moscow Patriarchate glorified this 'holy war'[46] and invoked Russia's traditional role as 'protector of holy sites' and Eastern Christians, others recalled the former alliance between the USSR and Baathist Syria.

Russia's intervention in Syria has revealed a new point of friction with Recep Tayyip Erdogan's Turkey, which is hostile to the Syrian regime. After several incidents, on 24 November 2015, a Russian bomber made an incursion into Turkish airspace before being shot down. Putin denounced this as 'a stab in the back', accusing the Turkish leadership of 'stuffing pockets ... and letting terrorists prosper from the sale of oil they stole in Syria'. He warned: 'We'll remind them of what they did, more than once. They'll regret it. We know what to do.'[47] In addition to economic and commercial sanctions, the Russians installed S-400 ground-to-air missiles in Syria, preventing Turkish flyovers. This antagonism between two regional powers briefly revived a disturbing memory: of the dozen or so wars fought between the Ottoman and Russian Empires from the sixteenth to the twentieth century, But the two leaders decided to mend fences. In the wake of the abortive overnight coup of 15–16 April 2016, Erdogan initiated unprecedented purges of the army and within education and other public sectors, while also targeting journalists. The regime slipped towards dictatorship and became increasingly vehement in its opposition to the European Union. Vladimir Putin has every interest in forging an alliance with another power hostile to 'decadent Europe'.

Really, nobody knows how Putin is going to develop his empire—where, when, or how he is going to act. What is certain, however, is that, thanks to certain Russian thinkers, he now has at his disposal a solid ideological basis for it, one that he expresses in his words and deeds. He will make tactical use of this doctrine, relying more heavily on one idea or another depending on how events unfold. Yet the essentials—empire and war—are sure to lie behind his future actions.

9

AN IDEOLOGY FOR EUROPE AND THE WORLD

Vladimir Putin has a plan for Europe and for the world, and he is convinced that he is not very far from achieving it. There are two components to this plan. The first is no less than 'the Russian world', while the second involves taking the lead in Europe's conservative movement—conservative in the Putinian sense, opposed to homosexuality, atheism, cosmopolitanism, the Internet and any expression of creativity, which is seen as a symptom of disorder.

The notion of the 'Russian world' first appeared in the nineteenth century with the earliest significant ideological justifications of the Russian Empire, and was reborn in the 1990s after the implosion of the Soviet system. In 2000, researchers identified a paradox in the contemporary Russian situation: 'Any country that aspires to the status of ... global power strives not only to satisfy the interests of its citizens, but must also work in the interest of the citizens of other states and countries. The more necessary Russia is to an important number of citizens of other states, the more Russia will hold a sustainable position in the world. Russian governance can and must seek to ground its durability and purpose within the limits of the Russian World, in a policy of constructive development of its global networks.'[1] Put plainly, Russia must look after those Russians who live in other states, even if they do not hold Russian citizenship.

This 'Russian world' has been shaped by the dramatic events that punctuated the twentieth century. The country was first emptied of a section of its elites during the 1917 revolution, then again at the end of the civil war and in the 1920s. A second wave of emigration took place in 1944–5. Dissidents and refuseniks followed in the 1970s and 1980s. In the 1990s, people left for economic reasons, and from the 2000s, young people left to study abroad and did not always come back. The brain drain was worrying. Millions of Russians were not living in Russia but instead were clustered in communities across the world. This phenomenon hit home among politicians: the Russians of the diaspora had to be won back.

As early as his first inaugural speech in 2000, Putin underlined the importance of 'protect[ing] Russian citizens everywhere—both inside and outside the country'.[2] He wasn't yet invoking the Russian world or the theme of Russian-speaking non-citizens, but the seed was sown. The following year, the president was offering blandishments to those attending the first Congress of Russian Compatriots Living Abroad. After the collapse of the Soviet Union, he said, émigrés and the descendants of émigrés had dreamt of rediscovering their place in the lost—or fantasy—'fatherland'. They were offered Russian passports. Some of the aristocrats among them claimed back the family properties confiscated during the revolution and were filmed for television in front of their former palaces. Figures from the world of culture were fittingly feted, while businessmen and professionals were offered new contacts and even projects. Putin sensed a force that needed harnessing. Thinking both of these former émigrés and of the Russian-speaking ex-Soviet citizens dispersed throughout the new republics, he declared: 'The Russian-speaking community, along with the citizens of Russia, make up a fifth of the world's population. There are tens of millions of people who speak, think and—perhaps most importantly—feel in Russian, but live beyond the borders of the Russian Federation.'[3]

Putin's objectives regarding these people would only become apparent over time. In 2004, on a visit to Cannes, Putin commended those Russian émigrés who had 'piously conserved our country's traditions and upheld by various means national culture and the Russian language, and always maintained spiritual links with Russia'. In the following years the 'Russian world' project was to be more clearly organized, and was officially launched in 2007. It was intended to go broader than the defence of Russian-speaking minorities in the former USSR or the glorification of White émigré cultural and spiritual values, and its central aim was the advancement of Russian speaking (2007 was made Year of the Russian Language). Embracing a romantic conception of language that was typically Slavophile, Putin announced in 2006 that Russian 'is not only the means of communication for the millions of people who speak it or know it. It is an encapsulation of our national spiritual wealth.'[4] He also promised concrete measures for its promotion. Several days earlier, he had encouraged the Russian-language journal *La Pensée russe*, historically published by the Russian émigrés in France and associated with anti-Soviet dissidence, to 'participate in the union of the "Russian world"—a world of science, knowledge, of rich history and tradition'.[5] It had been a few months since a new management team very faithful to the Putinian ideological line had taken over the reins.

In Moscow, meanwhile, the year 2007 also witnessed the appointment of Vyacheslav Nikonov as head of the Russkiy Mir (Russian World) Foundation. Nikonov was a historian close to the Kremlin, president of the Politika Foundation and a United Russia party deputy. Born in 1956, he is also none other than the grandson of Vyacheslav Molotov, Stalin's foreign minister and the signatory of the 1939 Nazi–Soviet pact; Nikonov has written a biography of him. Yet while the grandfather defended Stalinism around the world, the grandson's mission has been to make every Russian speaker living abroad a bearer of the Putinian vision of Russia. In practical terms, he has initiated programmes promoting Russian throughout the world, opening houses of Russian language and culture. He is also in complete agreement with the president's view of the world, stating at the 2010 World Political Forum that 'the Russian democratic model will be difficult to create. It will be neither American nor British: it will be typically Russian or it will not be anything.'[6] As for the West's supposed hostility towards Russia, Nikonov and Putin are on the same wavelength again; the former declared to *Pravda* in 2014, 'A war against Russia has been waged for a thousand years. Today is no exception. The West's struggle against Russia will never cease.'[7]

Another favoured vehicle for building the 'Russian world' is Orthodoxy. Putin was explicit at the 2007 ceremony for official reconciliation between the Moscow Patriarchate and the Russian Orthodox Church Abroad, which was founded in opposition to the Church's submission to the Bolsheviks: 'The restoration of unity in the Church is an essential prerequisite for the restoration of the lost unity of the entire Russian world, a world in which the Orthodox faith has always acted as a spiritual foundation.'[8] Quite another fate has been reserved for those Orthodox Churches that are unwilling to return to the Moscow fold, wishing to keep their political and spiritual independence. In 2003, a row broke out between the so-called Ecumenical Patriarchate of Constantinople, which controls the Russian Churches abroad, and its Moscow counterpart. In several European countries, Moscow then demanded the 'restitution' of churches and cathedrals built before the revolution, as in Nice in 2009, and elsewhere provoked changes in jurisdiction by influencing priests and congregations. A soft cultural policy had thus been transformed into a brutal offensive. In France, having failed to take control of Paris' Orthodox cathedral on rue Daru, the Russian authorities decided to build 'their' cathedral close to the Eiffel Tower, having already created an Orthodox seminary in the Parisian suburb of Épinay-sous-Sénart in 2009. The Russian state has created linguistic, economic, cultural or religious associations in order to turn Russian émigrés into completely docile agents of influence.

* * *

The other aspect of the export of Putinian ideology is the conservative message, addressed not only to Russian-speakers but to all European citizens. For the Kremlin, it's a closed case: Europe is in a state of economic decline and moral decadence. Putin believes that hostility towards Islam and the protests linked to same-sex marriage in France are of profound significance. From this a fantastical picture emerges, whereby a small group of ultra-modernists, inspired by American-style theories, are apparently surreptitiously seeking to impose reforms on the population that would lead to major anthropological changes, not least the suppression of reproduction. For Putin, this represents an important stage in the war of civilizations, and it is vital that Europe should be helped to remain faithful to its Christian roots and traditional values. In the spring of 2014, he claimed to have warned his 'friends' of the rise of populism in Europe, which he attributed to permissiveness with regard to immigration and gay rights: 'I have been telling my friends in Europe for years that if you continue like that, without taking into account the mood of the population in your own countries, then nationalism will rise inexorably. And that was what happened.'[9] The Russian conservative turn, then, must be exported, and Putin sees himself as the harbinger of that anti-modernist movement.

With this in mind, Russia implanted 'Institutes of Democracy and Cooperation' in New York and Paris in 2007. Their objective is to promote the values of the new Russia. And if they are obliged to respond to Western criticisms about respect for human rights in Russia, why shouldn't Russia in its turn monitor breaches of rights in these hypocritical countries that consider themselves beyond reproach? The official task of the Institutes is to 'study and evaluate the organization of the electoral process and the follow-up of elections; to encourage studies and the creation of efficient programmes aimed at countering xenophobia, racism, extremism and terrorism'.[10] Yet they also organize seminars and conferences around the main themes of the Kremlin's new doctrine: defence of a multipolar world against American hegemony, protection of the 'traditional family', and 're-information' on the war in Syria, events in Ukraine and so on. Their spokespeople are regularly invited by the media to provide a 'politically incorrect' counterpoint to 'Western propaganda'. The war of information that emerged with the annexation of Crimea and the separatist struggle in Ukraine is an essential vector for Russian influence. The Russia Today media group, operating in English, French and German, enjoys an annual budget of tens of millions of euros and in November 2014 launched an international news agency named Sputnik (replacing The Voice of Russia), while the German-language 'magazine for sovereignty' *Compact* is designed to spread the Kremlin's ideas across the Rhine.

The desire to raise the global profile of Russia as the motherland of conservatism can also be felt in the ever-closer ties established with far-right populist movements, in particular the French National Front. Putin has long wagered on the rise and eventual victory of Marine Le Pen, who is herself a great admirer of the Russian president. Le Pen's former diplomatic adviser Aymeric Chauprade, a great disciple of Eurasianism, was among the 'independent observers' who went to monitor the conduct of the Crimea referendum in March 2014, and led viewers of the Russia-1 TV channel to believe that France officially endorsed this role. Part of the former UMP (the party of Sarkozy, now Les Républicains) as well as the Front de Gauche (Left Front) have allegedly expressed approval of Putin as a 'strong man' who dares to stand up to the United States. Politicians like Thierry Mariani have not concealed their backing for Putin and the annexation of Crimea. The Russian president's audience in Europe has undoubtedly grown.

Here is just one example of Putin's support for the most radical conservatives: in August 2014, he welcomed to Yalta, Crimea the Eurosceptic, Islamophobic and ultra-conservative politician Philippe de Villiers, who leads the Mouvement pour la France. What clearly interested Putin above all was not a man marginal to the French political scene but the fact that in February that year his brother had become the French Army's chief of the defence staff. Yet he was also pleased by any gesture suggesting approbation of his annexation of the peninsula, and was interested in the idea of developing a historical theme park there, similar to de Villiers' Puy-du-Fou attraction in France's Vendée region.

Russia was eager to turn Crimea, now a federal subject of Russia, into a zone open to casinos; at the end of April 2014, Putin introduced a bill adding Crimea to Russia's list of authorized 'gambling zones'. The bill was passed in May, casinos were soon under construction, and Crimea was in need of a more moral form of entertainment to complement it—Philippe de Villiers had arrived at just the right moment. He duly pledged allegiance to the new champion of conservatism: 'I want to say that in the hearts and minds of many Europeans, President Vladimir Putin is a much more respected figure, who they would much rather emulate than the majority of European leaders.' Putin was approving: 'It is true that quite a few people do share our views and approaches. We will continue on our road of course, defend our principles and our views, and rely on the people who share these views with us, whether in Russia, in France, or anywhere in the world.'[11] In other words, he awaits the rise to power of populist parties so that he can become Europe's leader—and to make this happen he has committed all necessary resources, financial and otherwise.

On top of the Russian intervention in the 2016 US electoral campaign [see Chapter 5], on 15 November 2017 the British government revealed that Russian online pirates, controlled by the Kremlin, had intervened in the 2016 EU referendum campaign that ended in a vote for Brexit. According to Ciaran Martin, head of the UK's National Cyber Security Centre, the Russian interference was on a massive scale: 45,000 messages were posted by Russian accounts in just forty-eight hours.[12] Accusing the Russian authorities of seeking to 'weaponize information', Prime Minister Theresa May declared: 'I have a very simple message for Russia. We know what you are doing. And you will not succeed.'[13]

At around the same time, suspicions crystallized of Russian intervention in the Catalan independence movement. An investigation by *El País* highlighted Twitter interventions from several Russian accounts, as well as from WikiLeaks founder Julian Assange—who has worked for Russian state television—and Edward Snowden, currently claiming political asylum in Russia.[14] These tweets affirmed that the EU would recognize Catalan independence, or compared the deteriorating situation in Barcelona with that of Tiananmen Square in spring 1989. A few weeks later, Spain's defence and foreign affairs ministers accused Russia-based 'entities' of running a disinformation campaign surrounding the 1 October Catalan referendum. Foreign Affairs Minister Alfonso Dastis cited fake Twitter accounts, half of Russian origin and 30 per cent from Venezuela—a Russian ally and debtor.[15]

For Vladimir Putin, anything that could serve to divide or weaken Europe should be encouraged. As the Trump White House contemplates a disengagement from Europe's defence in a rejection of NATO, Putin dreams of a continent on its knees, worn down by separatist movements and dominated by a new conservative leader: himself. He is lying in wait for the post-Merkel era, when he can make a bigger move. This approach is a subtle one. Instead of directly attacking his European neighbours, Putin encourages European populations to rise up against their leaders. He is sending a digital Trojan horse into a whole series of democracies, and encouraging their own citizens to make use of them. Even more cunning than Ulysses, the Russian president appears to have convinced the Trojans to overthrow Priam and sack the city themselves.

Ultimately, the different parts of Putinian ideology fit together perfectly. In order to construct the broadest possible Eurasian empire, Putin must mobilize the Russian population around the idea of a particular historic 'way'. And to sway the rest of the world to his advantage, he has decided to make himself the champion of an anti-modernist and archeo-conservative paradigm. In so doing he also remains faithful to his Soviet heritage. During the twentieth century, the USSR had worked, with some success, to install or maintain friendly regimes, to support fraternal parties, to win hearts and minds, to pass off the Soviet version of communism as the only great emancipatory dream worth defending. But with the collapse of the Soviet Union, Russia had to resign itself to becoming a country like any other, neither better nor worse. Since then, thanks to the most nationalist and pseudo-scientific elements of Russian philosophy, Putin has given back his country its international ideological vocation. Under his rule, identity-based conservatism is to act as a beacon for all the world's peoples, and conservative mobilization, initiated and directed by the Kremlin, will no longer know borders. The USSR was not a country, but a concept. In Putin's hands, Russia is once again the name of an idea.

NOTES

INTRODUCTION: PUTIN AND PHILOSOPHY

1. Natalya Galimova, 'Berdyaev Putin-style', Gazeta.ru, 16 May 2014.
2. Website of the All-Russian Popular Front, 18 August 2014.
3. Vladimir Putin, speech at the 'Business and Globalization' summit, Brunei, 15 November 2000. Almost all of Putin's speeches can be found, in Russian and English, on the website of the Russian presidency, Kremlin.ru.
4. Vladimir Putin, 'Russia at the Turn of the Millennium', an article published on 30 December 1999 in various newspapers, available at pages.uoregon.edu/kimball/Putin.htm, last accessed 19 October 2017.
5. Vladimir Putin, meeting with students at Kaliningrad University, Kaliningrad, 27 June 2003.
6. Anton Vaino, Anton Kobyakov and Victor Saraev, *The Image of Victory*, Institute for Economic Strategies RAN, 2012, p. 83. Vernadsky is very famous in Russia and Putin referred to him during a speech in November 2000.
7. See Charles Clover, 'Putin and the Monk', *FT Magazine*, 25 January 2013.

1. SOVIETS FIRST AND FOREMOST

1. Vladimir Putin, interview on US TV channel NBC, 2 June 2000. http://en.kremlin.ru/events/president/transcripts/24204
2. As explained in Masha Gessen, *The Man without a Face: The Unlikely Rise of Vladimir Putin*, London: Granta, 2013.
3. Vladimir Putin, conversation with cultural actors, Yalta, 14 August 2014.
4. Vladimir Putin, interview, NBC, 2 June 2000.
5. Vladimir Putin, interview, BBC, 5 March 2000.
6. Vladimir Putin, interview, NBC, 2 June 2000.
7. Ibid.
8. Svetlana Alexievich, *La Fin de l'homme rouge*, Arles: Actes Sud, 2013, p. 149.
9. Ibid, p. 109.
10. Ibid, p. 46.
11. Vladimir Putin, speech, 9 May 2012, during the parade commemorating the sixty-seventh anniversary of victory in the Second World War.
12. Vladimir Putin, interview, NBC, 2 June 2000.
13. Ibid.
14. Ibid.
15. Testimony of his friend Sergei Roldugin, quoted in Putin's first authorized biography, *First Person: Conversations with Vladimir Putin*, by Natalya Gevorkyan, Natalya Timakova and Andrey Kolesnikov (*Ot pervogo litsa: Razgovory s Vladimirom Putinym*, http://archive.kremlin.ru/articles/bookchapter1.shtml).
16. Vladimir Putin, interview, *Le Figaro*, 26 October 2000.

17. Declaration on the modification of national symbols, 4 December 2000.
18. Ibid.
19. https://wciom.ru/index.php?id=236&uid=115661
20. https://www.levada.ru/2017/02/14/fevralskaya-revolyutsiya-1917/
21. *Direct Line* with the readers of the daily *Komsomolskaïa Pravda*, 9 February 2000.
22. Vladimir Putin, address to Federal Assembly, Kremlin, Moscow, 25 April 2005.
23. Vladimir Putin, interview, *Time*, 19 December 2007.
24. Vladimir Putin, Presidential Address to the Russian Federation, Moscow, 18 March 2014. My emphasis.
25. Interview, NBC, 2 June 2000.
26. Vladimir Putin, 'Russia at the Turn of the Millennium', an article published on 30 December 1999 in various newspapers. See pages.uoregon.edu/kimball/Putin.htm
27. He has roundly criticized it, for instance during an interview with the Russian TV channel ORT on 15 January 2000.
28. Vladimir Putin, interview with daily *Gazeta Wyborcza* and Polish TV channel TPV, 15 January 2002.
29. 'A statue of Felix Dzerzhinsky has been unveiled in Kirov', RBK, 7 September 2017, http://www.rbc.ru/rbcfreenews/59aee3359a7947ce7da05b20 (last accessed 10 November 2017); 'Felix Dzerzhinsky Museum opening on 11 September', Kirov Portal, 26 July 2017, https://kirov-portal.ru/news/poslednie-novosti/muzej-feliksa-dzerzhinskogo-otkroyut-11-sentyabrya-23163/ (last accessed 10 November 2017).
29. Alexander Morozov, interview with the author.

2. KANT, PETER THE GREAT AND THE PHILOSOPHY OF JUDO

1. Fyodor Dostoevsky, *Notes from Underground*, London: Alma Classics, 2010.
2. Vladimir Putin, interview, *Bild*, 18 September 2001.
3. Alexander Morozov, interview with the author.
4. Vladimir Putin, speech at the inauguration of a memorial to Kant, University of Kaliningrad, 3 July 2005.
5. Vladimir Putin, Kremlin meeting with German Minister of Foreign Affairs Joschka Fischer, Moscow, 12 February 2004.
6. Putin, speech at the inauguration of memorial to Kant.
7. Masha Gessen, *The Man without a Face: The Unlikely Rise of Vladimir Putin*, London: Granta, 2013, Chapter 4.
8. Ibid. 'Putin and Sobchak shared the same antipathy for the democratic process, but at the beginning of the 1990s a display of allegiance to these principles was the price for access to public life.'
9. Vladimir Putin, interview with daily *Gazeta Wyborcza* and Polish TV channel TPV, 15 January 2002.
10. Morozov, interview with the author.
11. Putin, interview with *Gazeta Wyborcza*.
12. Ibid.
13. Ibid.
14. Vladimir Putin, interview, BBC, 5 March 2000.
15. Ibid.
16. Vladimir Putin, press conference, Madrid, 14 June 2000.
17. Vladimir Putin, interview with French TV channels TF1 and France 3, 23 October 2000.
18. Ibid.
19. Vladimir Putin, interview, TF1, 11 February 2003.

20. Ibid.
21. Vladimir Putin, meeting with members of the Valdai Club, Novo-Ogaryovo, Moscow region, 25 October 2012, transcript available at http://en.kremlin.ru/events/president/news/16717 (last accessed 24 October 2017).
22. Andrei Illarionov, interview with the author.
23. Ibid.
24. Ibid.
25. Ibid.
26. Ibid.
27. Ibid.
28. Vladimir Putin, interview with Chinese newspaper *Renmin Ribao* (People's Daily), New China news agency and RTR television channel, 16 June 2000.
29. Ibid.
30. Vladimir Putin, interview with *India Today* and *Russia Journal*, 29 September 2000.
31. Vladimir Putin, speech to participants and guests, European judo championship, 25 April 2013.
32. Vladimir Putin, interview with Japanese TV channel Fuji Terebi, 4 July 2000.
33. Putin, interview with *India Today*.

3. THE PRESIDENT'S FIRST PHILOSOPHICAL LOVE

1. After the Bolshevik revolution of October 1917, a civil war pitted the Red Army led by Leon Trotsky against the tsarist 'Whites', who would be defeated in 1923 and then emigrate throughout the world, especially to France.
2. See the article entitled 'Ilyin's Day', *Kommersant*, 29 May 2006.
3. Vesti.ru, 24 May 2009.

4. Nikolay Mitrokhin, interview with the author.
5. Quoted in Basil Zenkovsky, *Histoire de la philosophie russe*, vol. II, Paris: Gallimard, 1955, p. 390.
6. In August 1922, Lenin had several hundred intellectuals opposed to the Bolshevik revolution arrested. That autumn they were deported on two vessels nicknamed 'the philosophers' ships'. Among them were some of Russia's greatest thinkers, such as Sergei Bulgakov, Semyon Frank, Nikolai Berdyaev, Lev Karsavin, Roman Jakobson and so on.
7. Ivan Ilyin, *O soprotivlenii zlu siloju* (*Resistance to Evil by Force)*, Chapter XVIII, 1925, in *Sobranie sotchinenij*, Moscow: Russkaya kniga, vol. 5, 1996, p. 168.
8. Nikolai Berdyaev, 'Kochmar zlogo dobra' ('The Nightmare of an Evil Good'), in *Put'*, no. 4, June–July 1926, pp. 103–16, English translation available at http://www.berdyaev.com/berdiaev/berd_lib/1926_312.html (last accessed 25 October 2017).
9. Ivan Ilyin, 'National Socialism. A New Spirit. I', in *Stat'i, lektsii, vystupleniya, retsenzii (1906–1954)*, Moscow: Russkaya kniga, 2001, p. 322.
10. I.A. Ilyin, 'O fachisme' ('On Fascism'), 6 December 1948, extract from *Nachi zadatchi (Our Mission)*, in *Sobranie sotchinenij*, vol. II, book I, Moscow: Russkaya kniga, 1993, p. 89.
11. Mitrokhin, interview with the author. The links between fascism, national socialism and part of the White émigré community are complex and little known. Was there a 'Russian fascism', anti-democratic and anti-communist, but also modernist? The question is still open. Whatever the truth, Putin's discourse has revived the debate. See, in

this respect, Walter Laqueur, *Black Hundreds: The Rise of the Extreme Right in Russia*, New York: HarperCollins, 1993.

12. Nikita Mikhalkov, *The Russian Philosopher Ivan Ilyin*, 2011, 47 minutes. In this television film, Nikita Mikhalkov, with his seductively husky voice, emphasizes what, in his view, matters in Ilyin's work: his critique of the liberals, of the 'formal democrats' responsible for the revolution and incapable of understanding Russia, and of the 'semi-intellectuals' cut off from the essential qualities of the Russian people. The film ends with a call for a strictly centralized and vertical form of power. It must be said that the film was broadcast in the midst of a period of political upheaval in early 2012.
13. Vladimir Putin, 'Annual Address to the Federal Assembly of the Russian Federation', The Kremlin, Moscow, 25 April 2005, http://en.kremlin.ru/events/president/transcripts/22931 (last accessed 25 October 2017).
14. Ibid.
15. Ibid.
16. Ibid.
17. Ivan Ilyin, 'The Principal Task of a Future Russia', *Our Mission*, in *Sobranie sotchinenij*, Moscow: Russkaya kniga, 1993, p. 265.
18. Ibid., p. 278.
19. Vladimir Putin, 'Annual Address to the Federal Assembly', Moscow, 10 May 2006, http://en.kremlin.ru/events/president/transcripts/23577 (last accessed 25 October 2017).
20. Ibid.
21. Vladimir Putin, speech, Kremlin, Moscow, 26 June 2013.

General Alexander Suvarov (1730–1800) was an 'invincible' military leader who drastically improved conditions for all ranks of soldier in the imperial army.

22. Ilyin, 'Optimizm v politike' ('Optimism in Politics'), *Our Mission*, book I, p. 85.
23. *Ilyin*, 'Predstojachtij v Rossii khaos', ('The Chaos to Come in Russia'), *Our Mission*, book I, p. 20.
24. *Ilyin*, 'Natsionalnyj vojd i partijnye glavari' ('The National Guide and the Leaders of Parties'), *Our Mission*, book I, p. 35.
25. Vesti.ru, 24 May 2009.
26. Ilyin, *Our Mission*, book I, pp. 326–40.
27. Ibid.
28. Ilyin stood for a different concept of freedom. According to him, 'Whoever loves Russia must aspire to its freedom. Above all freedom for Russia itself, its international independence and autonomy. Secondly, freedom for Russia understood as the unity between Russians and all other national cultures. And finally, freedom for Russians, for all of us: freedom in faith, in the search for truth, in creation, in work and in property.' Ilyin, 'Rossii neobkhodima svoboda' ('Freedom is Indispensable to Russia'), *Our Mission*, vol. II, book I, p. 163. In his address to the Federal Assembly on 4 December 2014, Putin quoted these words from Ilyin and spoke of their 'enormous meaning'.

4. THE CONSERVATIVE TURN

1. Vladimir Putin, meeting with students at Irkutsk State University, 18 February 2000.
2. Vladimir Putin, interview with TV Channel One and

Associated Press, Novo-Ogaryovo, Moscow region, 4 September 2013, http://en.kremlin.ru/events/president/news/19143/ (last accessed 30 October 2017).
3. Vladimir Putin, interview with German TV channels ARD and ZDF, 9 June 2000.
4. Vladimir Putin, interview with daily *Gazeta Wyborcza* and Polish TV channel TPV, 15 January 2002.
5. Vladimir Putin, interview with New China news agency and CCTV TV channel, Moscow, 27 November 2002.
6. Ibid.
7. Vladimir Putin, Federal Council for Development of Russian Culture, St Petersburg, 16 June 2003.
8. Vladimir Putin, meeting with French journalists, Bordeaux, 12 February 2003.
9. Vladimir Putin, speech to participants at meeting of the Bishops' Council of the Russian Orthodox Church, Moscow, 6 October 2004.
10. Vladimir Putin, interview, *TIME*, 19 December 2007.
11. Ibid.
12. The term 'near abroad' (*blizhneye zarubezhiye*) is commonly used in Russia to refer to the fourteen other former Soviet republics.
13. See Marlène Laruelle, *Russian Nationalism and the National Reassertion of Russia*, London: Routledge, 2010.
14. Vladimir Putin, meeting with Patriarch Alexy II, Peredelkino, Moscow region, 13 Augusr 2004.
15. Vladimir Putin, press conference with Russian and foreign media, Kremlin, Moscow, 1 February 2007, http://en.kremlin.ru/events/president/transcripts/24026 (last accessed 30 October 2017).
16. Putin, interview, *TIME*.

17. Vladimir Putin, speech at meeting of Presidential Council for Culture and Art, Kremlin, Moscow, 30 May 2007.
18. Vladimir Putin, speech to the Russian Literary Assembly, Moscow, 21 November 2013.
19. Vladimir Putin, speech, ceremony for the bicentenary of the Battle of Borodino, 2 September 2012.
20. Ibid.
21. Vladimir Putin, speech at meeting on patriotic education, Krasnodar, 12 September 2012, transcript available at http://en.kremlin.ru/events/president/news/16470 (last accessed 30 October 2017).
22. Vladimir Putin, Presidential Address to the Federal Assembly, Kremlin, Moscow, 12 December 2012, http://en.kremlin.ru/events/president/news/17118 (last accessed 30 October 2017).
23. Vladimir Putin, meeting of the Valdai International Discussion Club, Novgorod region, 19 September 2013. http://en.kremlin.ru/events/president/news/19243 (last accessed 30 October 2017).
24. See the Russian daily, *Vedomosti*, 25 September 2013.
25. Putin, meeting of the Valdai Club.
26. 'I can call myself a pragmatist with a conservative perspective,' he stated in the decisive autumn of 2013. Putin, interview with TV Channel One and Associated Press.
27. Vladimir Putin, Presidential Address to the Federal Assembly, Kremlin, Moscow, 12 December 2013, http://en.kremlin.ru/events/president/news/19825 (last accessed 1 November 2017).
28. RIA Novosti news agency, 12 February 2014.
29. Stanislav Khatuntsev, 'The Russian Jupiter', Russian Idea, 5 June 2014, http://politconservatism.ru/thinking/russkiy+yupiter/ (last accessed 30 October 2017).

30. Boris Mezhuev, interview with the author.
31. Konstantin Leontiev, 'Byzantinism and Slavdom', in *Vostok, Rossia i Slavianstvo* (The East, Russia, and Slavdom), Moscow: Republika, 1996, p. 152.
32. Konstantin Leontiev, 'The Average European as an Ideal and Instrument of Universal Destruction', in *Vostok, Rossia i Slavianstvo* (The East, Russia, and Slavdom), Moscow: Republika, 1996, p. 426.
33. Putin, meeting of the Valdai Club.
34. Nikolai Plotnikov, interview with the author.
35. Carl Schmitt, *The Concept of the Political*, Chicago IL: Chicago University Press, 1996.

5. THE RUSSIAN WAY

1. Vladimir Putin, address to State Duma deputies, Federation Council members, heads of Russian regions and civil society representatives, Kremlin, Moscow, 18 March 2014, http://en.kremlin.ru/events/president/news/20603 (last accessed 30 October 2017).
2. Miranda Green, 'Putin: Trump appeared to agree Moscow did not interfere in election', CNN, 8 July 2017, http://edition.cnn.com/2017/07/08/politics/putin-trump-election-interference/index.html (last accessed 3 November 2017).
3. Jason Horowitz, 'Steve Bannon Cited Italian Thinker Who Inspired Fascists', *The New York Times*, 10 February 2017, https://www.nytimes.com/2017/02/10/world/europe/bannon-vatican-julius-evola-fascism.html?_r=0 (last accessed 3 November 2017).
4. Vladimir Putin, televised speech, 24 March 2000.
5. Vladimir Putin, speech on 'the two thousandth anniversary of the birth of Christ', Kremlin, Moscow, 11 January 2000.

6. Vladimir Putin, discussion with journalists during a journey to Solovetsky Islands, Arkhangelsk district, 20 August 2001.
7. Vladimir Putin, interview, *The Wall Street Journal*, 11 February 2002.
8. Vladimir Putin, interview, NBC, 2 June 2000, http://en.kremlin.ru/events/president/transcripts/24204 (last accessed 30 October 2017).
9. Vladimir Putin, press conference with Russian and foreign journalists, Kremlin, Moscow, 23 December 2004.
10. Vladimir Putin, Presidential Address to the Federal Assembly, Kremlin, Moscow, 25 April 2005.
11. Vladimir Putin, meeting with members of the Valdai International Discussion Club, Sochi, 14 September 2007, http://en.kremlin.ru/events/president/transcripts/24537 (last accessed 30 October 2017). English translation slightly modified for clarity.
12. Ibid.
13. Vladimir Putin, Presidential Address to Federal Assembly, Kremlin, Moscow, 12 December 2013, http://en.kremlin.ru/events/president/news/19825 (last accessed 30 October 2017).
14. Vladimir Putin, speech to participants at a meeting of the Bishops' Council of the Russian Orthodox Church, Kremlin, Moscow, 1 February 2013.
15. Vladimir Putin, interview with makers of the film *The Second Baptism of Rus*, 23 July 2013. http://en.kremlin.ru/events/president/news/18872 (last accessed 30 October 2017).
16. Vladimir Putin, Presidential Address to the Federal Assembly, Kremlin, Moscow, 12 December 2012, http://

en.kremlin.ru/events/president/news/17118 (last accessed 30 October 2017).

17. Alexander Solzhenitsyn, 'Kak nam obustroit' Rossiiu?' ('How Shall We Reorganize Russia?'), pamphlet, 1990.
18. Vladimir Putin, interview with TV channels ORT and RTR and daily *Nezavissimaya Gazeta*, 25 December 2000.
19. Alexander Solzhenitsyn, quoted in Bertrand Le Meignen, *Alexandre Soljenitsyne. Sept vies en un siècle*, Arles: Solin/Actes Sud, 2011, p. 829.
20. Vladimir Putin, speech, Kremlin, Moscow, 12 June 2007.
21. Ibid.
22. Vladimir Putin, Presidential Address to the Federal Assembly, Kremlin, Moscow, 10 May 2006, http://en.kremlin.ru/events/president/transcripts/23577 (last accessed 30 October 2017).
23. Presidential decree, 28 June 2014.
24. P. Chaadayev, *Lettres philosophiques adressées à une dame*, 'Lettre première', *Œuvres complètes*, vol. I, p. 93, (*Polnoe sobranie sotchinenij i izbrannye pis'ma*, t. I, Moscow: Nauka, 1991).
25. Ibid, p. 96.
26. Ibid, pp. 96–7.
27. Alexei Khomiakov, 'Neskol'ko slov o *Filosofitcheskom pis'me* napetchatannom v 15 knijke *Teleskopa*' ('Some words on the *Lettres philosophiques* published in the 15th issue of *Teleskop*'), www.vehi.net/khomyakov/izpisma.html (last accessed 30 October 2017).
28. I.V. Kireevsky, *Polnoe sobranie sotchinenij*, Moscow, 1911 (republished by Gregg International Publishers Limited, Farnborough, Hants, 1970), vol. I, p. 112.

29. Ibid., p. 113.
30. '"Moscow raised the banner of all Russia and became a capital," wrote the historian and philosopher Konstantin Aksakov.' Vladimir Putin, speech at ceremonies consecrated to the 860th anniversary of the founding of Moscow, Moscow, 2 September 2007.
31. Nikolai Plotnikov, interview with the author.
32. Nikolai Berdyaev, *Khomiakov*, Lausanne: L'Âge d'homme, 1990, p. 49.
33. Ibid., p. 50.
34. Ibid., p. 52.
35. Alexandre Koyré, *La Philosophie et le problème national en Russie au XIXe siècle*, Paris: Gallimard, 1975, p. 13.
36. Ibid., p. 15.
37. Plotnikov, interview with the author. Admittedly, some of Ukraine's believers look to the Moscow Patriarchate, which is allied with the Kremlin. But not all were supporters of Putin and they have pleaded for Church neutrality in the conflict between pro-Russians and pro-Europeans. Furthermore, the rest of Ukraine's Orthodox Christians are tied to the Kiev Patriarchate, or the Autocephalous Church, which has been autonomous since the 1920s.
38. N. Danilevsky, *Rossia i Evropa (Russia and Europe)*, St Petersburg: Glagol, 1995, p. 339. English translation published by Slavica Publishers (Bloomington IN, 2013).
39. Ibid., p. 368.
40. Hegel, *Elements of the Philosophy of Right*, Cambridge: Cambridge University Press, 1991, p. 361.
41. Danilevsky, *Russia and Europe*, p. 371.
42. Ibid., p. 373.

43. Ibid., pp. 389–90.
44. Ibid., p. 390.
45. Ibid., p. 407.
46. Berdyaev, *Khomiakov*, p. 106.

6. THE EURASIANIST DREAM

1. Vladimir Putin, speech, Moscow, 6 December 2002.
2. Vladimir Putin, *Nezavissimaya Gazeta*, 14 November 2000.
3. Vladimir Putin, investiture speech, Kremlin, Moscow, 7 May 2012. http://en.kremlin.ru/events/president/news/15224 (last accessed 31 October 2017).
4. Vladimir Putin, Presidential Address to the Federal Assembly, Kremlin, Moscow, 12 December 2013, http://en.kremlin.ru/events/president/news/19825 (last accessed 31 October 2017).
5. Vladimir Putin, meeting with the Kazakh president Nursultan Nazarbayev, Kremlin, Moscow, 15 May 2012.
6. Vladimir Putin, meeting with the Seliger 2014 National Youth Education Forum, 29 August 2014, http://en.kremlin.ru/events/president/news/46507 (last accessed 31 October 2017).
7. See Marlène Laruelle, *La Quête d'une identité impériale. Le néo-eurasisme dans la Russie contemporaine*, Paris: Petra, 2007, p. 13.
8. The title of a Savitsky text published in 1927.
9. See Marlène Laruelle, *L'Idéologie eurasiste russe*, Paris: L'Harmattan, 1999, p. 152.
10. Pyotr Savitsky, ('Geografitcheskie i geopolititcheskie osnovy evrasijstva' ('The Geographical and Geopolitical Foundations of Eurasianism'), 1933, available in the orig-

inal Russian at Gumilevica.kulichki.net (last accessed 31 October 2017).

11. See Nikolai Trubetzkoy, 'Russkaïa problema' ('The Russian Problem'), 1921; available in *Nasledie Tchingiskhana*, Moscow: Agraf, 1999, p. 341.
12. Nicolai Trubetzkoy, ('Vzgliad na russkuju istoriu ne s zapada, a s vostoka', ('Russian History Seen Not From the West but From the East', available in *Nasledie Tchingiskhana*, Moscow: Agraf, 1999, p. 230.
13. On the avatars of neo-Eurasianism in contemporary Russia, see Laruelle, *La Quête d'une identité impériale*. It should be recalled that Alexander Dugin was co-founder, with Eduard Limonov, of the National Bolshevik Party in 1993.
14. The Organisation armée secrète, or Secret Army Organisation, was a pro-French Algeria far-right paramilitary group, which carried out terror attacks during Algeria's war of independence (1954–62).
15. Particularly, he was a faithful friend of Éric Rohmer. See Antoine de Baecque and Noël Herpe, *Éric Rohmer: A Biography*, New York: Columbia University Press, 2018.
16. Alexander Dugin, *La Quatrième Théorie politique*, Nantes: Ars Magna, 2012, p. 54.
17. Ibid., p. 62.
18. Ibid., p. 165.
19. Ibid., p. 166.
20. Ibid., p. 225.
21. Ibid., p. 228.
22. Alexander Dugin, interview with the author.
23. Alexander Morozov, interview with the author.
24. Vladimir Putin, speech at a meeting of professors and stu-

dents of L.N. Gumilev Eurasian National University, Astana, 10 October 2000.

25. Vladimir Putin, speech at an international forum on 'Eurasian Integration', Astana, 18 June 2004.
26. Vladimir Putin, speech at the celebration of Kazan's millennial anniversary, Kazan, 26 August 2005.
27. Vladimir Putin, address to a congress on Gumilev, St Petersburg, 1 October 2012.
28. Vladimir Putin, interview, *Socium*, no. 5, 1992.
29. See Laruelle, *La Quête d'une identité impériale*.
30. Vladimir Putin, Presidential Address to the Federal Assembly, Kremlin, Moscow, 12 December 2012, http://en.kremlin.ru/events/president/news/17118 (last accessed 31 October 2017).
31. Morozov, interview with the author.
32. Vladimir Putin, meeting of the Praesidium of the Council for Culture and Art, Pskov, 3 February 2014.
33. Morozov, interview with the author.

7. FALSE FRIENDS: DOSTOEVSKY AND BERDYAEV

1. Vladimir Putin, interview with Polish media, 15 January 2002.
2. Vladimir Putin, interview with *Paris Match*, 6 June 2000.
3. Vladimir Putin, speech at the inauguration of the statue of Fyodor Dostoevsky, Dresden, 10 October 2006.
4. Ibid.
5. Vladimir Putin, '50 Years of the European Integration and Russia', 25 March 2007. http://en.kremlin.ru/events/president/transcripts/24094 (last accessed 1 November 2017).
6. Dmitir Bykov, 'Osboe mennie' ('Special Opinion'), Echo of Moscow radio, 26 May 2014, https://echo.msk.ru/

programs/personalno/1326764-echo/ (last accessed 3 November 2017).

7. Russian Idea website: http://politconservatism.ru/forecasts/ne-znayu-yavlyayus-li-ya-konservativnym-fantastom-no-kak-chelovek-ya-konservator/.
8. Fyodor Dostoevsky, *A Writer's Diary*, November 1877, 3.1, Evanston, IL: Northwestern University Press, 1993, p. 790.
9. N. Danilevsky, *Rossia i Evropa* (*Russia and Europe*), St Petersburg: Glagol, 1995, p. 420.
10. Fyodor Dostoevsky, *The Adolescent*, New York: Knopf Doubleday, 2007, p. 469.
11. Dostoevsky, *A Writer's Diary*, p. 526.
12. The term used by Dmitri Karamazov to characterize 'Russian man'.
13. See Mikhail Bakhtin, *Problems of Dostoevsky's Poetics*, Minneapolis, MN: University of Minnesota Press, 1984.
14. Fyodor Dostoevsky, letter to Konstantin Pobedonostsev, 19 May 1879.
15. Vladimir Putin, Presidential Address to the Federal Assembly, Kremlin, Moscow, 12 December 2013, http://en.kremlin.ru/events/president/news/19825 (last accessed 1 November 2017).
16. Boris Mezhuev, interview with the author.
17. Quoted in the magazine *Korrespondent*, 18 February 2014.
18. Nikolai Berdyaev, 'Has There Been in Russia a Revolution?', *Narodopravstvo*, 19 November 1917, http://www.berdyaev.com/berdiaev/berd_lib/1917_284.html (last accessed 1 November 2017).
19. Ibid.

20. Nikolai Berdyaev, 'Philosophical Verity and Intelligentsia Truth', in Berdyaev, Nikolai, *Vekhi: A Collection of Articles about the Russian Intelligentsia* (trans., ed. Sergei Bulgakov et al), Armonk NY: M.E. Sharpe, 1994, available at https://archive.org/stream/ BerdiaevNikolai VekhiLandmarks ACollectionOfArticlesAboutTheRussian Intelligentsia/ Berdiaev, %20Nikolai%20-%20Vekhi%20 Landmarks% 20%20A%20Collection%20of%20Articles% 20About% 20the%20Russian%20Intelligentsia_djvu.txt (last accessed 1 November 2017).
21. Nikolai Berdyaev, *Filosofiia neravenstva* (*The Philosophy of Inequality*), Paris: YMCA Press, 1970, p. 88.
22. Nikolai Berdyaev, *Dostoevsky: An Interpretation*, London: Sheed & Ward, 1936.
23. This correspondence was published at our initiative in no. 74 of *Philosophie Magazine* (November 2013) and translated into English translation partly taken from in *Comradely Greetings: The Prison Letters of Nadya and Slavoj*, London: Verso 2014.
24. Berdyaev, *The Philosophy of Inequality*, p. 93.

8. PUTIN'S EMPIRE

1. Vladimir Putin, meeting with members of the Valdai Club, Sochi, 14 September 2007. http://en.kremlin.ru/events/president/transcripts/24537 (last accessed 1 November 2017).
2. 'Abkhazia is recognized—by Nauru', *The New York Times*, 15 December 2009.
3. *Süddeutsche Zeitung*, 18 September 2014.
4. Barack Obama, 'Remarks to the People of Estonia', Nordea Concert Hall, Tallinn, 3 September 2014, https://obama-

whitehouse.archives.gov/the-press-office/2014/09/03/remarks-president-obama-people-estonia (last accessed 1 November 2017).

5. Alexander Prokhanov, interview with the author.
6. On this subject, see the very powerful writing of the Georgian philosopher Merab Mamardashvili in *La Pensée empêchée* (*Hindered Thought*), a collection of interviews with Annie Epelboin (La Tour-d'Aigues: Éditions de l'Aube, 1991). According to Mamardashvili, 'totalitarian language and totalitarian society create a language which excludes waking ... You can ... die without ever discovering what *your* feeling was.' Thinking for one's self is replaced by 'thought-on-your-behalf, for you'. It is the totality of the being that is hence confiscated. Mamardashvili recalls: 'When I was young, people from the Komsomol ran the body social and mine too: they managed my body.' This killing of thought produced what he called 'a life from beyond the grave' in a 'forest of walking corpses'.
7. See Svetlana Alexievich, *La Fin de l'homme rouge (Second-Hand Time)*, Arles: Actes Sud, 2013, p. 149.
8. Vladimir Putin, 'Interview for the documentary film *The Second Baptism of Rus*', 23 July 2013. http://en.kremlin.ru/events/president/news/18872 (last accessed 3 November 2017).
9. Lenta.ru, 20 November 2008.
10. Interfax news agency, 5 May 2011.
11. Interfax news agency, 17 December 2010.
12. Lenta.ru, 27 September 2011.
13. Father Vsevolod Chaplin, interview with the author.
14. Vladimir Putin, press conference, Moscow, 19 December

2013. http://en.kremlin.ru/events/president/news/19859 (last accessed 3 November 2017).
15. Vladimir Putin, interview with New China news agency and CCTV TV channel, Moscow 27 November 2002.
16. Vladimir Putin, speech at ceremony marking the beginning of construction of the Alexander Pushkin Russian-Turkmen School, Ashgabat, 11 May 2007.
17. Ibid.
18. Andrei Illarionov, interview with the author.
19. Vladimir Putin, speech at meeting of teachers and students at the L.N. Gumilev Eurasian National University, Astana, 10 October 2000.
20. Putin, meeting with members of the Valdai Club.
21. Vladimir Putin, speech at a meeting of Presidential Council for Culture and Art, Kremlin, Moscow, 25 November 2003.
22. Vladimir Putin, press conference, Dushanbe, Tajikistan, 5 July 2000.
23. Vladimir Putin, interview with Chinese newspaper *Renmin Ribao* (*People's Daily*), New China news agency and RTR television channel, 16 June 2000.
24. Illarionov, interview with the author.
25. Nikolai Plotnikov, interview with the author.
26. I.A. Ilyin, *Nachi zadatchi* (*Our Mission*), in *Sobranie sotchinenij*, vol. II, book I, Moscow: Russkaya kniga, 1993, p. 125.
27. See Marlène Laruelle, *L'Idéologie eurasiste russe*, Paris: L'Harmattan, 1999, p. 16: 'The Eurasianists denied Ukrainians the right to self-determination: in a naturalist discourse it is irrelevant to consider such a question (does one ask whales to self-determine to know whether they are mammals or fish?).'

28. Vladimir Putin, speech at a reception marking the tenth anniversary of Ukraine's independence, Kiev, 23 August 2001.
29. Vladimir Putin, speech at the opening ceremony of the Year of Russia in Ukraine, Kiev, 27 January 2003.
30. Vladimir Putin, speech at a medal award ceremony for cultural figures, Kiev, 28 January 2003.
31. Vladimir Putin, press conference with Ukrainian president Leonid Kuchma, Yalta, 4 May 2003.
32. Vladimir Putin, press conference with Russian and foreign journalists, Kremlin, Moscow, 23 December 2004.
33. Vladimir Putin, meeting with Ukrainian president Viktor Yanukovych, Novo-Ogaryovo, Moscow region, 22 October 2012.
34. Vladimir Putin, press conference, Moscow, 20 December 2012.
35. Vladimir Putin, meeting with Ukrainian president Viktor Yanukovych, Tver, Tver region, 4 March 2013.
36. Vladimir Putin, meeting with representatives of different Orthodox Patriarchates and Churches, Kremlin, Moscow, 25 July 2013, http://en.kremlin.ru/events/president/news/18942 (last accessed 3 November 2017).
37. Vladimir Putin, meeting with Ukrainian president Viktor Yanukovych, Kiev, 27 July 2013.
38. Vladimir Putin, metting of the Valdai International Discussion Club, Novgorod region, 19 September 2013, http://en.kremlin.ru/events/president/news/19243 (last accessed 3 November 2017).
39. 'Direct Line with Vladimir Putin', annual special TV programme, Moscow, 17 April 2014, http://en.kremlin.ru/events/president/news/20796 (last accessed 3 November 2017).

40. Kirill Lipatov, interview with the author.
41. Alexander Morozov, interview with the author.
42. Vladimir Putin, meeting with the Seliger 2014 National Youth Education Forum, 29 August 2014. http://en.kremlin.ru/events/president/news/46507 (last accessed 3 November 2017).
43. Vladimir Putin, meeting with students from Lomonosov Northern (Arctic) Federal University, 9 June 2014, http://en.kremlin.ru/events/president/news/45881 (last accessed 3 November 2017).
44. Voice of Russia, 16 October 2014.
45. *The Moscow Times*, 1 October 2014.
46. Interfax news agency, 30 September 2015.
47. Vladimir Putin, Presidential Address to the Federal Assembly, Kremlin, Moscow, 3 December 2015, http://en.kremlin.ru/events/president/news/50864 (last accessed 3 November 2017).

9. AN IDEOLOGY FOR EUROPE AND THE WORLD

1. 'Russkij mir. Vozmojnye tseli samoopredelenija' ('The Russian World: Possible Objectives of Self-Determination'), Russkij Arkhipelag website, http://www.archipelag.ru/authors/shedrovicky_petr/?library=2015 (last accessed 3 November 2017).
2. Vladimir Putin, inauguration speech, Kremlin, Moscow, 7 May 2000, available in the original Russian at kremlin.ru/events/president/transcripts/21399 (last accessed 3 November 2017).
3. Vladimir Putin, opening speech, first Congress of Russian Compatriots Living Abroad, Moscow, 11 October 2011.

4. Vladimir Putin, introductory remarks, meeting of 'creative intelligentsia', St Petersburg, 26 November 2006.
5. Vladimir Putin, interview with *La Pensée russe*, 23 November 2006.
6. Vyacheslav Nikonov, contribution to discussion on the theme of 'Standards of democracy and the diversity of democratic experiments', second World Political Forum, Yaroslavl, 9 and 10 September 2010.
7. *Pravda*, 8 April 2014.
8. Vladimir Putin, speech at the Ceremonial Signing of the Act on Canonical Communion of the Moscow Patriarchate and the Russian Orthodox Church Abroad, 17 May 2007.
9. Vladimir Putin, meeting with management of world press agencies, St Petersburg, 24 May 2014.
10. Statutes of the Institute of Democracy and Cooperation.
11. Vladimir Putin and Philippe de Villiers (Mouvement pour la France leader), meeting, 24 August 2014, http://en.kremlin.ru/events/president/news/46454 (last accessed 3 November 2017).
12. Alex Hern, 'Russian hackers targeted UK media and telecoms firms, confirms spy chief', *The Guardian*, 15 November 2017, https://www.theguardian.com/technology/2017/nov/15/russian-hackers-targeted-uk-media-and-telecoms-firms-confirms-spy-chief (last accessed 24 November 2017).
13. Rowena Mason, 'Theresa May accuses Russia of interfering in elections and fake news', *The Guardian*, 14 November 2017, https://www.theguardian.com/politics/2017/nov/13/theresa-may-accuses-russia-of-interfering-in-elections-and-fake-news (last accessed 24 November 2017).

14. David Alandete, 'La maquinaria de injerencias rusa penetra la crisis catalana', *El País*, 25 September 2017, https://politica.elpais.com/politica/2017/09/22/actualidad/1506101626_670033.html (last accessed 24 November 2017).
15. Jennifer Rankin, 'Catalan independence: EU experts detect rise in pro-Kremlin false claims', *The Guardian*, 13 November 2017, https://www.theguardian.com/world/2017/nov/13/catalan-independence-eu-experts-detect-rise-in-pro-kremlin-false-claims (last accessed 13 November 2017).